The Development of Adaptive Intelligence

A Cross-Cultural Study

Carol Fleisher Feldman

Benjamin Lee

James Dickson McLean

David B. Pillemer

James R. Murray

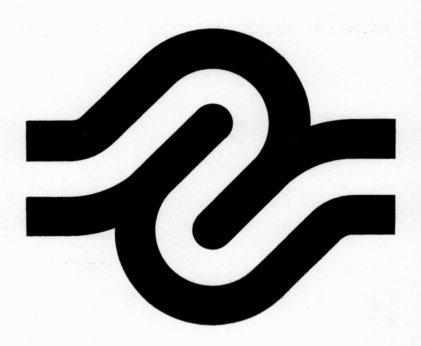

THE DEVELOPMENT
OF ADAPTIVE
INTELLIGENCE

 Jossey-Bass Publishers
San Francisco · Washington · London · 1974

THE DEVELOPMENT OF ADAPTIVE INTELLIGENCE
A Cross-Cultural Study
     by Carol Fleisher Feldman, Benjamin Lee, James Dickson McLean,
     David B. Pillemer, and James R. Murray

Copyright © 1974 by: Jossey-Bass, Inc., Publishers
                 615 Montgomery Street
                 San Francisco, California 94111
                              &
                 Jossey-Bass Limited
                 3 Henrietta Street
                 London WC2E 8LU

Library of Congress Catalogue Card Number LC 73-22557

International Standard Book Number ISBN 0-87589-224-8

Manufactured in the United States of America

JACKET DESIGN BY WILLI BAUM

FIRST EDITION

Code 7412

The Jossey-Bass
Behavioral Science Series

*To the children
of the North Slope*

Preface

$\mathbb{I}$n *The Development of Adaptive Intelligence* we look at logical thought as a product of man's adaptation to his environment. The central focus is a study of the development of thinking in the Eskimo. In particular we use a specially constructed nonverbal test of logical thinking to examine the Piagetian hypothesis that development has the same hierarchical structure in all cultures undergoing successful adaptation.

Although the project as a whole was meant to be a serious contribution to psychological theory, the present account has been organized so that it can be read profitably by anyone interested in the nature of development, in cross-cultural research, or in the culture of the Eskimo people. The theoretical and methodological framework is discussed in the first chapter. For the specialist, the statistical details of the methodology are presented in some detail in the Appendix. Chapter Two contains a basic account of Piagetian theory, a critical discussion of past work in the field, and specific suggestions about how to test the theory. Also, the goals

Preface

and problems of cross-cultural Piagetian research are discussed in the context of examples. Chapter Three is an ethnographic sketch of the culture of the Eskimo villages we visited during the research. The fourth chapter describes the test used in the research. Chapter Five contains the model underlying the hypothesis of hierarchical structure and the data that support it. In the last chapter the implications of the research for psychological theory and for Eskimo education are discussed.

The research produced strong evidence that the development of thought can be conceived of as a universal, invariant sequence of stages. We argue that Piaget's theory provides a useful way to conceptualize this structure as the necessary outcome of an adaptive process that leads the developing person toward an increasingly effective interaction with his environment.

Chicago
January 1974

Carol Fleisher Feldman
Benjamin Lee
James Dickson McLean
David B. Pillemer
James R. Murray

Acknowledgements

The research reported here developed over the five years from 1969 to 1973. I am deeply indebted to the many people who provided major assistance. R. Darryl Bock of the University of Chicago provided the initial opportunity to go to the North Slope of Alaska, and I had the valuable experience, rare in the life of junior professors, of learning an area from someone with more experience. Fred Milan of the University of Alaska supported this research in every imaginable way—with the excellent rapport he established in the Eskimo villages, with the food and places to stay that he magically arranged, with transportation, with support for assistants, and especially with his extensive knowledge of the people of the North Slope and of the management of field research.

Benjamin Lee, Dickson McLean, and David Pillemer, who were centrally involved in conceptualizing the problem and who also participated in the field work, can never be adequately thanked for their patience, endurance, and wisdom over a period of years. James Murray was unusually helpful as a statistical con-

Acknowledgements

sultant, and his interest in the research led him to develop new and original analytical techniques which were especially appropriate for the somewhat unusual questions we were asking.

In addition, I am in great debt to the three generations of students who gave lavishly of their time to various aspects of the research. I would like especially to thank Addison Stone, who transformed an unreadable manuscript into one which is hopefully now readable. I would also like to thank Robert Berlin, who ran the Kentucky sample, Karen Silverman, who searched the literature for us, Daniel Osherson, who was centrally involved in the design of the board test described in Chapter Two, and Spencer Swinton, who was similarly responsible for the design of the machine test, also described in Chapter Two. Julian Henriquez did a professional job of computer management for the analysis of the data.

I am greatly indebted to the villagers of Point Hope, Wainwright, Anaktuvik Pass, and Barrow for their many kindnesses; to the Naval Arctic Research Laboratory in Barrow for logistical support; to the International Biological Program, Human Adaptability subsection, sponsored by the United States Public Health Service, for financial support in the field; to the National Laboratory for Early Childhood Education, Early Education Research Center, of the Office of Education, for support in the data analysis; and to the superintendent of the Mount Edgecumbe School, Sitka, Alaska, and the principal of the Hindman Settlement School in Kentucky for permitting and facilitating our visits.

The final preparation of this manuscript was managed by Sandra Schwartz, to whom I am especially grateful for conscientiousness in an extremely tedious job.

CAROL FLEISHER FELDMAN

Contents

Contents

The Development
of Adaptive
Intelligence

A Cross-Cultural Study

1

Intelligence as Adaptation

The present research began in 1969 in response to a request made on behalf of the Human Adaptability section of the International Biological Program, a large, multinational study of circumpolar peoples. We were asked to develop psychological evidence relevant to the goal of the larger study. That goal was to define the behavioral and biological mechanisms and processes associated with the unique adaptation of the Eskimos in the hostile environment of northern Alaska. We interpreted this as a request to investigate the thinking abilities of the Eskimos, and in particular the organization and generativity of their conceptual processes.

The difficulty of the task we had undertaken became increasingly apparent in subsequent years, as we were forced to recognize the many problems associated with the administration of earlier tests. The largest problem was that the most reliable tests of intellect are not directed toward the adaptive properties of thought, but instead are tests of a particular conception of intelligence.

The various tasks used in most intelligence tests are selected on the grounds of high predictiveness for each other. That is, it is believed that there is a common factor which includes these various performances, at least within a common culture. The magnitude of this common factor varies widely among individuals, and intelligence tests are designed to reveal these individual differences.

Although we hoped to investigate stable, basic characteristics of intelligence, we were not interested in revealing individual differences. In fact, we hoped to measure characteristics of intelligence so necessary to survival that they would not vary strikingly among healthy, adequately functioning individuals. At this very early stage, we were already doubtful of the usefulness of the more psychometric approaches to intelligence.

In the early years, we thought that standard tests might be used if we did away with the assumption that they test a common factor of underlying intelligence. Vernon's pioneering work (1969) used batteries of standard tests in foreign cultures in this way. Rather than assuming that those tests tapped a general underlying potential, he thought that each culture would have a distinctive pattern of relations among the tests—a pattern which could be used to characterize that culture. For example, one group might be found to be high in verbal ability and low in spatial ability, and another to be just the reverse.

Vernon's use of the tests differed from the standard use in ways that were helpful. It permitted some reasonable conclusions to be drawn about the mental abilities of people in foreign cultures through the use of standardized tests. Unfortunately, the very same reconceptualization which made Vernon's use of the tests helpful for some purposes—that is, for thinking of the various tests as measuring different abilities—made it useless for

2

ours. We were after something more general. Moreover, we did not want to know about acquired ability but rather about a latent potential to cope which would help in difficult and variable circumstances.

Even when measures of intelligence are used to draw inferences about underlying potential, they do so by measuring acquired ability. For example, knowledge of vocabulary, which is the best predictor of the total intelligence score, is obviously learned. The inference from learned skills to underlying potential is made by assuming equal exposure in all members of the population to the skill in question. More intelligent people, then, through greater ability to learn, would learn more.

The equal exposure assumption is responsible for many current problems in the use of intelligence tests within our own culture. It obviously invalidates their use outside of it. We rarely are in a position to assess whether people living under circumstances different from our own have had experiences equal to, greater than, or less than ours with knowledge in any particular area. So we are unable to interpret high scores as revealing anything more than that a great deal has been learned; we cannot infer great learning potential, or the converse. But it was the learning potential that we were after.

A main reason for rejecting the psychometric approach is that in that approach the abilities investigated are not tied to a general theory of adaptation. As a consequence, the results of research following such an approach can in no way be interpreted as indicating anything about universal properties of thought, or about the unique nature of the adaptive aspect of human intelligence. We wanted to emphasize this adaptive aspect of intelligence.

Our interest in intelligence as adaptation led naturally to a consideration of Piagetian theory. Much of the power and utility of Piaget's characterization of cognitive development is due to his explicit formulation of intelligence as a particular form and extension of universal processes of biological adaptation. Intelligence is not a bundle of cognitive abilities. It is a process that extends the range of biological adaptation from the play of instincts to the broader reaches of symbolic thought. The cognitive structure that evolves in this way is not a mere epiphenomenon of the biological structure by which it may be at least partly controlled; it is a level of description of the organism without which no understanding of what it is to be human would be complete.

If we believe that biological processes characterize humans, it is because the adaptive interaction involved in those processes provides a mechanism that ought to operate universally. In isolating cognitive characteristics as candidates for universality, we need to provide a similar mechanism. Cognitive processes that are claimed to define humanness must appear, regardless of the inevitable variations in both environment and constitutional endowment.

The power of Piaget's characterization of cognitive development lies in its provision of a universal mechanism for cognitive development. Given a normal constitution and a normal environment, the child is said to follow Piaget's hypothesized progression by means of continuous dynamic interaction. The newborn infant interacts actively with his environment. Through this process, the reflexes with which he is born differentiate and evolve into slightly more elaborate structures called *schemata*. These are the earliest mental organizations and the precursors of all later ones.

In Piaget's view, these schemata finally form structures which give the young child a distinctive way of organizing the world. The child uses these structures to interact with an ever-expanding environment, and this process leads to a reorganization of the structures of the first stage. This new stage subsumes the structures of the earlier stage, so that the stages are hierarchically arranged and must inevitably succeed in order. The new organization pervades the child's thinking at the next stage, and it is with this new structure that he explores his newly conceived world.

It should be evident, even from this simple description,

that Piagetian theory provides a mechanism of development that allows us to conceive of the developmental organization of mental processes as universal. Every viable human is born with reflexes, and every child has an environment to try them out on. The universal result is an inevitable progression of cognitive structures.

If Piagetian theory characterizes universal processes, it is obviously an important model for understanding cognitive development. As such it has been used by many researchers, most notably by Piaget himself. Its value for those studying cognitive development cross-culturally was even more obvious. Rather than selecting for testing skills that are valued or common in the culture of the investigator, we could at last identify abilities which might be presumed to be of some greater significance. If Piagetian processes are universal, it follows that they are of adaptive value and are therefore of considerable importance.

Despite the longevity of Piagetian theory, it is only in the past decade or so that researchers have set out to establish the universal presence of its characteristic processes; however, they have made up for lost time. Literally hundreds of studies purporting to be Piagetian have been done in foreign cultures (Dasen, 1972).

As with most very good things, there was a serious problem. Piaget's evidence had been gathered by a clinical method of flexible questioning. The child was given an interesting situation to think about, and then Piaget asked him such questions about it as were necessary to determine the quality of the child's thought. This was unpalatable to experimentally-minded American psychologists, who preferred controlled and standardized procedures. In addition, it was impossible to use this method in most cross-cultural situations. Not uncommonly, the investigator could not speak the local language well enough, and the children were unwilling to describe their thinking to an adult.

Piaget had studied a set of mental organizations, called *conservation,* by methods that seemed relatively easy to standardize. Moreover, although Piaget had placed his greatest reliance on the children's explanations of their choices, it looked as though those explanations might be bypassed by scoring the child's choices alone. The materials could even be arranged so that the children could make their choices by pointing. Many studies have been done using materials in this way. Such studies enable an investigator to infer that those children who answer in particular ways are probably at a particular operational level.

Nevertheless, there is reason for dissatisfaction with these techniques. Often it is not possible to conclude, on the basis of performance, that the stage being tested was attained by subjects. Children may fail for bizarre reasons (see Greenfield, 1966). Furthermore, conservation at one stage might not be a distinctive indicator for thinking in that stage (see Wilkinson, Lunzer, and Dolan, 1973). As if to reinforce this doubt, various results have begun to show large differences in conservation ability within a stage, depending on the characteristics of the materials being conserved. The crowning blow was provided by studies that showed that the most advanced kind of conservation was not revealed by using these same techniques in our own culture (Hall and Kingsley, 1968).

This series of developments led some investigators to conclude that conservation, and therefore all of Piagetian structure, was not universal but rather depended on environmental influences. It led others to abandon conservation and to attempt to test constructs more central to the theory.

Rather than studying the stage-characteristic structures of thought (such as conservation) in and of themselves, the present research was addressed to the issue of whether thought structures characteristic of the various Piagetian stages evolve according to the developmental pattern that Piaget has described—that is, whether they are hierarchically arranged. It is intrinsic to Piaget's conception that such development is an interactional process whose form is the same in all cultures. To examine this aspect of the theory, it is necessary to validate the hierarchical nature of development in at least some cultures different from our own.

To operationalize the research goals, a simple nonverbal test sequence was designed to tap cognitive abilities across the

Piagetian stages with the same stimuli, a simple set of colored blocks, for problems at all levels. Only in this situation can one produce evidence adequate to confirm the proposed hierarchy of stages. To do this, it is not enough to give a battery of tests; it is crucial that the test sections be interrelated by a logical hierarchy of increasing complexity. If such complexity is to be the only variable, the same materials and procedures must be used for all of the tasks. Thus, each successive task builds on the skills and materials of its predecessor, and failure at any level can only be attributed to the absence of the operational ability at issue.

As a preliminary attempt to assess universality, the test was given to the Eskimo children of a village in Alaska's remote North Slope. Because Piaget's theory predicts that adaptation will always take the form of a hierarchically organized sequence of abilities, evidence from well-adapted cultures must show the presence of such a structure. It would not have been enough to show hierarchical structure without universality, or universality in the absence of hierarchical structure, because of the interactional bases on which Piaget's model rests.

Our research strategy is somewhat unorthodox, but for good reason. In standard psychological research where quantitative measures are used, it is possible to evaluate measurement error by using error variance. When the measures are qualitative, however, it is difficult to measure reliability (Murray, Wiley, and Wolfe, 1971). We tackled this problem at two levels—statistical and methodological. First, an analysis procedure was devised that makes a preliminary attempt to estimate measurement error as well as to test validity through an elaborate item analysis (see Appendix).

Second, a methodology was employed that required a gamble—both the test and the theory had to be operating to obtain positive results. Although negative evidence would have been impossible to interpret, finding a hierarchical structure of development among the Eskimos was substantiation of the validity of both the theory and the test. It was, nonetheless, possible that some strange interaction of an invalid test and the Eskimo cul-

7

ture produced spurious positive results. To eliminate this possibility, the test sequence was given to the children of a rural Kentucky hill town. The further corroboration obtained there makes it unlikely that the Eskimo results are due to a strange interaction. We are left, then, with evidence for the universal and hierarchical nature of the adaptational process Piaget calls intelligence.

2

Piagetian Theory in Cross-Cultural Research

This chapter presents the background of the research. The first part presents our interpretation of Piaget's theory, particularly those aspects to which our research was directed. The second and third sections place the present research within the context of previous Piagetian and cross-cultural testing. The final section outlines our preliminary attempts to handle the problems discussed in the preceding two sections.

Theoretical Framework

Piaget believes that human cognition results from an interaction between organismic endowment and environmental encounters. This now classical observation is relevant to our task

9

and, indeed, to all studies of cognitive development, because it indicates the inevitable difficulty of isolating particular constitutional or environmental factors as adequate accounts of adaptation. The research reported here was not designed to measure the effect of environmental variation on the development of intelligence. It contrasts with much cross-cultural research in which, for example, cognitive abilities of two groups of children —who are from the same culture but who experienced different kinds of schooling—are compared. Hence, only the most tentative efforts are made here to account for the nonuniversal aspects of thinking observed in our sample. Just as causes cannot be located in particular environmental factors, so they cannot be located in biological endowment. Our interactionist perspective is that the finding of universals in cognitive structure does not imply purely biological causation. Rather, we believe that culture-invariant principles are resultants produced by a particular form of biological adaptation of organism to environment which repeatedly throughout the life span creates the abilities observed on any occasion of testing. It is consistent with this perspective to take the view that certain adaptive aspects of intelligence are universally important and might be expected to emerge in all cultures, or at least in all successfully adaptive cultures.

Piaget conceives of intelligence as a particular form of biological adaptation between the organism and the environment. The organism is an open system constantly interacting with the environment, trying to maintain a fit between its own needs and the demands that the outside world makes on it. If the adaptation is successful, the survival chances and well-being of the animal are enhanced; if not, then it dies and the species as a whole may gradually die out. Cognition (or symbolic behavior) extends the scope of biological adaptation from the immediate present by internalizing and representing at the level of symbolic processes that which was previously only possible at the level of action. Overt trial and error, with its irreversible consequences, can be replaced by implicit trial and error, where the possible consequences can be mapped out before actual behavior takes place. Piaget (1963, p. 49) wrote:

> *As we have seen, we may represent the hierarchy of response patterns, right from the early reflexes and global perceptions, as a matter of progressively extending the distance and of progressively complicating the paths of interaction between the organism (subject) and the environment (object); thus each of these extensions or complications represents a new structure, while their succession is dependent on the need for an equilibrium which must be more and more mobile as it becomes more complex.*

Intelligence, as a particular form of biological adaptation dealing with the progressive articulation, coordination, and internalization of actions and their symbolic representations, is subject to the basic laws of biological adaptation. These basic laws of biological adaptation are called *functional invariants* and are of two kinds—organization, and the pair known as assimilation/accommodation.

Organization is, as Furth (1969, p. 263) explains, "the most general expression of the form of a biological organism, a totality in which elements are related to each other and to the whole, the totality itself being related to a greater totality." Another way of defining organization is to say that it is the tendency for organisms to systemize their processes into coherent subsystems (Ginsburg and Opper, 1969) that allow their progressive differentiation and coordination. The biological advantages of organization are numerous (see Simon, 1969). Every living system must have an organizational base in order to interact with its environment; without one, there would be no differentiation between organism and environment and hence no interaction.

Assimilation refers to that part of the organism-environment interaction which deals with the incorporation of the external stimulus into the organism's structure. This can occur at

11

the physiological level (for example, the incorporative aspects of digestion) or at the symbolic level (as in play). In assimilation, the organism is the independent variable and the environment is the dependent variable. Accommodation is that part of the organism-environment interaction which focuses on the adaptation of the organism's structures to features of the external environment. Thus, accommodation is the main process involved in imitation. In this case the organism is the dependent variable and the environment is the independent variable. The coordination of these two processes creates an equilibrium between organism and environment that is essential to a stable interaction between them.

In his study of cognitive development, Piaget has tried to characterize with logical models the various forms of equilibrium that thought can take. He calls these forms of equilibrium *structures,* and he views them as self-regulating systems of reversible transformations that form a totality, a whole which is greater than any of its parts (Piaget, 1970a and 1970b). Structures exist at two levels. The first is a *substantive* level, which consists of the units of the system under investigation. The second is a *formal* level, which consists of the principles (that is, reversible transformation) that structure and operate on the substantive units. The system can only be understood through a combined analysis of both levels.*

Much of Piaget's work has been concerned with the description and formalization of these formal and substantive units of the cognitive system as it develops in the individual. His research indicates that there are changes at both levels; these

---

* Piaget divides his system into two levels, the figurative and the operative, but these do not correspond to the formal/substantive division. The figurative level deals with the static accommodative aspects of cognition and includes perception and mental imagery, but not propositions. The division we have chosen is merely a heuristic to show the hierarchical organization of the stages; it is also a slight accommodation to the distinctions made by Chomsky (1965). A good discussion of the figurative/operative distinction, including why the figurative level is primarily accommodative, is found in Furth (1969).

changes are represented by structurally described stages that are posited to be universal. In the structural description, the lower stages are embedded in, and hierarchically subsumed by, the upper stages. The implication is that one must pass through the lower stages to reach the higher ones. Because the higher ones include the lower ones, one can think (in the structural sense of range of transformations) in the higher stages everything that one can think in the lower stages, and more; but in the lower stages, one cannot think everything that the higher stages make one capable of conceiving.

The substantive level develops from the construction of the concept of an object, to construction of a symbol, to construction of a sign, to construction of a proposition. The formal level that acts on these substantive units evolves from action, to the construction of simple one-way relations, to the development of transformations, to the structured transformation of the formal stage (the four-group formed by the operations of identity, negative, reciprocal, correlative [INRC]).

The hierarchical arrangement of the substantive level is quite elegant: In order to have a proposition, one must have signs, because a proposition is a relation between signs; in order to have a sign one must have a symbol to which it refers; in order to have a symbol one needs an object to which the symbol refers. The hierarchical nature of the formal level is similar. The INRC group is a system of four transformations and requires that there be an earlier development of transformations; transformations are, for Piaget, reversible relations which in turn develop from the simple relations; simple relations are abstracted coordinations of action, and thus, before there can be these coordinations, there must be actions to coordinate.

Using this formal hierarchical model, Piaget then proceeds to describe cognitive development as a sequence of four stages. At the first or sensori-motor stage, the child's abilities are limited to operating directly on objects without the mediation of any internal symbolic structures. The rather loosely defined abilities of the preoperational stage become active when the child is first capable of statically representing actions internally in the form of mental imagery. He becomes a primitive transformer of the environment, but his internal symbolic transformations remain unidirectional and therefore lack an internally consistent structure. With the onset of concrete operations, the child's internal actions become reversible; he is capable of mentally undoing what he has just done.

Concrete operations represent an advance from the preoperational period in that the child develops a complete, systematic scheme for organizing reality states. His conceptual apparatus is not, however, powerful enough to generate all of the possible combinations of propositions or all of the possible kinds of relations among relations. The ability to relate propositions into a coherent system containing the total array of propositional possibilities is the hallmark of formal operations. This stage takes the organized structures of concrete operations and spells out all their further inherent possible combinations when they are applied to such abstract subjects as propositions. At this level the child is able to reason about propositions independently of their truth or falsity; that is, he can consider them independently of the realities they stand for, and thus he is able to extend the range of his operations from particular responses to hypothetical propositions. (The reader familiar with Piaget's work on formal operations will have noted that little mention has been made of the structure of the formal abilities (the sixteen binary combinations and the INRC group). For the present purposes it was felt that being able to operate on propositions was a sufficient criterion to use as a measure of the onset of formal abilities.)

The Piagetian hypothesis that development is hierarchically organized into four stages can only be examined by using a test where the operations required at each level include those required at the lower level. The present research included construction of a test whose sections comprise a theoretically defined sequence of cognitive processes. The theoretical structure of the sequence is hierarchical; the ability measured by a test section assumes the existence of all preceding abilities. Using these materials, it was possible to consider the claim that cognitive development is hierarchically arranged. Furthermore, the test structure made possible a reasonably pure examination of the two empirically distinct hypotheses involved in Piaget's account of development: sequence and stage. Although these two hypotheses are in fact separable, they must be viewed as integral elements of the larger hypothesis for the purpose of theory validation. The existence of either one alone would not be sufficient evidence.

The sequencing hypothesis predicts that subject responses will conform to a pattern that reflects the hierarchical structure of the tasks; if a subject correctly responds on the test at some level, he will pass all easier tasks. Thus, the percentage of subjects who conform to one of the predicted sequencing patterns is a measure of the validity of the hypothesized sequential order of the abilities tested.

The stage hypothesis predicts that cognitive abilities appear dramatically and at increasingly higher age levels. Piagetian theory views the appearance of cognitive abilities as dependent on ontogenetic potential common to all mankind. The appearance of an ability should correspond to the age at which the potential to perform it is realized. Strong corroboration of the stage hypothesis would come from an analysis of subject performance on items versus age that demonstrates a distinct increase in the probability of a correct response at an age level. If, further, the abilities necessary to perform correctly on successive test sections appear at successively later age levels, that fact would further support the sequencing hypothesis.

In Piagetian theory, the nature of the structures in the particular stages is intrinsically related to the hierarchical nature of development of those structures, and so it is difficult to separate the two conceptually. Piaget's claim for the universality of his description of cognitive development may be taken as applying either to the stages or to their hierarchical arrangement. Moreover, it is difficult to separate empirically claims regarding the stages and their organization or development. Clearly, the hypothesized hierarchical developmental pattern would only be

15

demonstrable if some subjects were able to solve correctly problems requiring cognitive structures at all levels.

The present research is concerned with the hypothesis of the hierarchical arrangement of the structures characterizing the stages. Obtaining evidence for this structure in Eskimos as well as in more Westernized children not only would show that it can be demonstrated empirically but would also suggest that it is invariant across culture. Hence, Piaget's descriptions of the development of cognitive ability were used in a very special way. Rather than studying the structures of thought in and of themselves, the present research tests whether those thought structures evolve according to the developmental pattern which Piaget describes—that is, whether they are hierarchically arranged.

Testing Piagetian Theory

In an excellent survey of the Piagetian cross-cultural literature, Dasen (1972, pp. 23, 25) discusses the nature of research in this area:

> *Following the disappointing results of the "culture-free" and "culture-fair" movements, the attention of many cross-cultural cognitive psychologist[s] has turned to the developmental psychology of Jean Piaget (often called "genetic psychology"). The Piagetian psychologist is not concerned with the score on a test, but attempts to describe the basic structures and functioning of higher mental processes. He studies how the child gets to know about the world, how he develops basic scientific concepts, and how reasoning obeys certain structural properties which can be described by models drawn from logic and mathematics. It is thus interesting for the cross-cultural psychologist to determine whether these properties of thought, which are described by Piaget as basic to any knowledge, are universal or whether they are influenced by cultural factors.*

and further on:

Piagetian Theory in Cross-Cultural Research

Implicitly, or explicitly, most cross-cultural studies in genetic psychology ask whether cognitive development in non-Western cultures follows the same sequential succession of stages described by Piaget and by many other investigators in middle-class, Western children. And, if so, do these appear at approximately the same age levels?

Dasen goes on to say that there have been no studies of the succession of the three global stages, but rather that there have only been verifications of the presence of each stage independently from the others. The rest of the literature falls into two main categories: (1) "The successive acquisition of operations that bear on different contents, but obey identical structural laws: the so-called 'horizontal décalages' such as the sequence of the conservations of quantity, weight, and volume" and (2) "the sequence of substages on any particular test" (Dasen, 1972, p. 26).

As Dasen observes, there has not been a reported study of the aspects of Piagetian theory that are tested here—the succession of the three global stages. A study of the succession of the three global stages requires measures which use the same materials and procedures for all tested stages. A combination of tests that use new materials at each stage cannot readily be used to draw inferences regarding the structure of the developmental process. Although there have been some efforts of this kind (see below and the Annotated Bibliography), most cross-cultural Piagetian research focuses on a single stage, usually concrete operations as in (1) and (2) above (the décalage relations among various concrete operational skills, for example, conservation of number and conservation of quantity, and the substages in, for example, the conservation of liquid, from no conservation to partial conservation to conservation). Such tests do not measure the succession of global stages, nor even more than one stage, because failure on a conservation of quantity test, although it is considered to indicate preoperational thinking, is merely evidence of failure to demonstrate concrete operational thinking—there are not two distinct tests for the two stages.

17

The Development of Adaptive Intelligence

The preference for standard measures, stemming from the desire for comparability, has created a large body of literature concerned with testing for the existence of a single stage, or transition (for examples, see the Annotated Bibliography). Unfortunately, no one of the techniques that Piaget has described spans all of the main stages, and indeed most of the standard techniques can only be used to infer presence or absence of aspects of concrete operational thinking.

The dominant trend in cross-cultural Piagetian research has been to apply some test techniques that have been well described by Piaget himself, particularly techniques for testing conservation. These measures are usually considered to tap aspects of concrete operational thinking. When the procedures are adapted as standard and are used for testing in several cultures, instead of a different technique being devised for each culture tested, the results lend themselves more readily to cross-cultural comparisons. When such comparisons provide evidence for the existence of operational thinking in some cultures but not others, the failure to detect operational thinking is often interpreted as evidence for a developmental lag, although the same results might equally well be used to infer that operational thinking is not present in a particular culture. However, Piagetians tend to believe that the same underlying abilities are available everywhere. Cultural variations, in such factors as the age of appearance of abilities, are not central to Piagetian theory.

The studies using standard techniques have been more noteworthy for the intracultural comparisons they have enabled than for important discoveries stemming from cross-cultural contrasts. Several important studies have contrasted the effects of schooling and environment. The design of the Greenfield study (1966), for example, permitted comparison of urban and rural children, as well as of age groups. The impetus behind such studies is an attempt to find the locus in environmental factors of nonstandard responses to standard measures. This branch of cross-cultural cognitive studies is more Brunerian than Piagetian, because it replaces Piaget's interactionism with Bruner's greater emphasis on the role of environmental factors in accounting for cognitive development.

A wide variety of techniques have been used in various studies to measure the same underlying cognitive abilities. Perhaps the most noteworthy commonality among the various studies is the extent to which the authors agree that the Piagetian structures are underlying abilities which may be mapped in a wide range of equivalent tasks. One salient example of this perspective is the Price-Williams study (1961), which utilizes culturally familiar materials and in which the tester was himself fluent in the native language. The research presented here was strongly influenced by Price-Williams' view that the cognitive abilities described by Piaget may be accurately mapped in a variety of ways, and that the usual cultural modes should be taken into account in creating tasks. Such considerations may be extended beyond materials and language to create a setting that is comfortable. Greenfield, for instance, notes that she tried to minimize the effects of the strangeness of the individual test situation by having the children manipulate the test materials themselves. In the present study, the main setting problem is that the clinical method preferred for Piagetian testing could not be used because of the discomfort felt by Eskimo children in explaining their thought processes.

Studies by Pascual-Leone (1970), Pascual-Leone and Smith (1969), and Nassefat (1963) are the only ones known to us which attempt not simply to demonstrate the presence of single stages, but rather to demonstrate the developmental pattern across the stages that Piaget describes. These attempts will be discussed in some detail so that the strengths and weaknesses we see in them can be used to clarify our approach.

Thinking of intelligence as having to do with the "transformation of information and its coordination," Pascual-Leone analyzed the kinds of tasks used in research to determine a child's stage of cognitive development. He found that all of the tasks which are performed successfully by children of a given age are essentially equivalent with respect to informational complexity.

The Development of Adaptive Intelligence

On the basis of this finding, Pascual-Leone suggested that the Piagetian conception of intelligence corresponds roughly to what information theory might call *computing space*.

Subjects were presented with a series of simple, visual stimuli and were taught to respond to each stimulus with an overlearned motor behavior, such as raising a hand. Subjects of different ages were taught different numbers of stimulus response pairs; five-year-old subjects learned five such pairs; seven-year-olds learned six pairs, nine-year-olds learned seven pairs, and eleven-year-olds learned eight pairs. In the testing phase of the experiment, the subjects were presented with a series of compound stimuli. Each stimulus in the series was created by combining two or more of the stimuli for which responses had previously been learned. The compound stimulus was seen for five seconds, and after each stimulus presentation the subjects were expected to respond with as many of the appropriate motor behaviors as they could manage. The results of the experiment show regular increases with age in the number of stimulus elements that the children can handle. These results are interpreted as evidence for the existence of a central computing space that increases in size during maturation. Differences in the informational complexity of tasks that children at different Piagetian stages can successfully perform are attributed by Pascual-Leone to age-related differences in the size of this hypothesized central computing space.

Pascual-Leone's research is similar to the research reported here in that it is concerned with testing the validity of a developmental hypothesis rather than with attempting to determine what stage of development a subject has reached. However, although Pascual-Leone seems to think of qualitative differences in the abilities characteristic of the various Piagetian stages as being epiphenomenal to quantitative differences in the size of a central computing space, in the research reported here, the various stages are thought of as being qualitatively different.

Nassefat's thesis (1963) was discovered during the final stages of preparation of this book. It comes the closest to meeting

20

our criterion for a true test of the hierarchical sequence of stages and provides a good opportunity to clarify our goals. Nassefat tested 150 children aged nine to thirteen on six Piagetian tests. The tests included conservation of volume, verbal reasoning, probability, proportionality, and coordination of spatial displacements. Each consisted of several subtasks. The subtasks of a given test were not necessarily at the same operational level because some of the subtasks were used to introduce the others. Nassefat classified the reasoning used by the children in their answers in terms of the operational abilities required for a correct solution, rather than using performance on the tests as whole entities as his dependent measure. His procedure was to group together the subtasks of a given operational level to create task-batteries at each level. He found three levels: concrete, formal, and intermediate. The intermediate class included subtasks for which it was impossible to specify clearly the nature of the logical operations necessary for solution.

Two scoring methods were used for the analysis: a dichotomous (pass/fail) scoring and a four-level operational scale. In each case, Nassefat relied on group averages rather than individual responses. With both methods, he found the task-batteries of increasing difficulty (decreasing percent of correct responses for the group as a whole) in the predicted order of concrete, intermediate, and formal. This constituted his evidence for the sequencing hypothesis.

Nassefat used a measure of homogeneity of response across tasks of a given level (operationalized in several ways), in combination with a logical analysis of the tasks, to define the presence of a stage. He then looked for evidence of a succession of the form: (1) homogeneity, (2) heterogeneity, and (3) homogeneity of response across tasks. He expected to find the same sequence for both concrete and formal stages. This succession was his stage measure. It was predicted under the assumptions that: (1) well before the ages of acquisition of a stage, the responses will be uniform because everyone will fail; (2) as the stage is emerging, some tasks will be passed and some failed; and

(3) when the stage has been fully acquired there will be uniform success on all tasks. The nine-year olds were found to be at a maximum of homogeneity on the concrete tasks. Nassefat concluded that his age sample had not tapped the preceding heterogeneity. The thirteen-year olds seem to be approaching a maximum of homogeneity on the formal tasks, and Nassefat concluded that the formal stage fully appears somewhat thereafter.

Nassefat's suggestion that the measure of homogeneity (commonly operationalized as task intercorrelations) should show a developmental trend as a stage "comes in" is important in the light of current Piagetian research. Many studies have tried to test Piaget's concept of stage by looking for correlations among tasks for groups of subjects averaged over age. In the light of Nassefat's argument, this procedure is clearly not sufficiently sensitive.

It is clear that Nassefat was concerned with the notions of stage and sequence as the proper measures of Piagetian theory. His operationalizations of them were quite different from our own, however (see Chapter Four). In the case of stage, he chose to look at the structured cluster of abilities that Piaget considers to be a central criterion. We chose to look for a rapid emergence of a stage-characteristic ability as evidence for staging. These are two equally important criteria for identifying stages. Although we are willing to accept Nassefat's measure of stage, his sequencing measure must be considered inadequate. The hypothesis of invariant sequence is meant to apply to each and every individual and not to the group average. Nassefat used the latter, and it is well known that the group average need not reflect the behavior of its individual members. This is especially true in a case in which a large number of measures are used.

There are several additional shortcomings in Nassefat's study. His tasks were radically heterogeneous, he tested only two stages, he used a very narrow age range, and he sampled from a Western group. When comparing performance on two tasks believed to tap different abilities, it is crucial that the only difference between the tasks is the difference in operational level of performance demanded. Variations in format or material merely cloud the performance with unnecessary problems, such as stimulus familiarity. A more rigid examination of the theory would look for staging and sequencing across more than two stages, because the chance of finding disconfirming evidence would be much greater. The necessity for a broad age sample was made clear by Nassefat's inability to trace the total onset of either the concrete or the formal stage. Finally, the claims for universality inherent in Piaget's model cannot be tested with a Western sample.

Nassefat's research was an admirable attempt to get at the crucial aspects of Piagetian theory, and the study is in many ways a model of how to do such research. However, it did not permit verification of the central hypothesis that cognition is organized in an invariant sequence of stages.

Problems and Issues

The domain of cross-cultural testing can be discussed in terms of two nested distinctions. The first is the distinction between theory-testing and subject-testing. The second is the issue of cultural invariance or cultural relativity. The present research falls under the first half of each dichotomy: it is concerned with the testing of a theory of cultural invariance.*

When the goal of a cross-cultural study is assessment of the abilities of subjects, the research usually involves the administration of a task to the subjects in a sample drawn from an exotic population. The results establish a relation between the task and

* The present approach of looking for invariance is a research strategy based on a particular hypothesis and does not reflect a view of the exclusive importance of cross-cultural similarities. Indeed, in the present research some aspects of the results are not expected to be the same across cultures. However, in the present context, accounting for the locus of those differences in either maturational or environmental factors must at best be tentative. An understanding of this and of the other interesting and important differences between cultures would be of great value, and certainly of no less importance than the discovery of universals, but it was not undertaken here.

the subject. That relation may provide information concerning either the task or the subject, depending on which of the two is better known to the researcher. When the subjects have known characteristics, results will be seen as bearing on the task; when the tasks have known characteristics, the results may be seen as a valid expression of subject ability.

Culturally correlated differences in test performance resulting from such procedures are open to a variety of interpretations. They are usually interpreted in terms of one of two general positions or perspectives: (1) a relativistic perspective, and (2) a universalist perspective. Each of these two perspectives gives rise to interesting problems for research.

A relativistic interpretation of culturally correlated differences in test results assumes that such differences accurately reflect differences in the abilities that the test is designed to measure. Members of different cultures differ with respect to a number of easily observable dimensions, such as test performance. Thus, it is not unreasonable to assume that they also differ with respect to a number of less easily observable dimensions, such as underlying abilities.

Proponents of cultural relativism infer essential differences from superficial ones and are faced with the task of accounting for these essential differences. Relativists, then, are often interested in discovering and explicating genetic or experiential influences that might be responsible for essential differences—differences in general and underlying ability—between members of different cultures.

Relativistic interpretations of culturally correlated differences in test results are rejected by proponents of a universalistic perspective. Universalists are inclined to believe that members of different cultures are essentially similar with respect to general and underlying ability; hence, differences in test performance are superficial differences only, and should not be interpreted as evidence of differences in underlying ability.

Related to the universalistic belief in essential similarity is a reluctance to infer, from the poor performance of virtually all out-group subjects on virtually all in-group tests, the general incompetence of out-group subjects. Out-group subjects frequently give evidence, in their daily activities, of abilities that are not detected by in-group tests designed to assess those very abilities. For any group that fails to demonstrate concrete operations in a testing situation, extensive observation will probably indicate the use of analogous processes in their daily lives. People may not be at a single operative level in all domains. Rejecting as they do the notion that out-group subjects are generally incompetent, universalists attempt to discover culturally correlated differences that might be responsible for the poor test performance of out-group subjects. For example, in-group and out-group subjects may be differentially familiar with test materials or test content, or with the language of administration for the test.

Because it is possible to interpret the results from either of two somewhat contradictory perspectives, it is obvious that cross-cultural testing with the emphasis on the tested sample is an activity in which the locus of confidence is ambiguous between tests and subjects. In contrast, the evaluation of theory is a reasonably straightforward process. A theory is propounded, and some testable hypothesis is derived from it. A task or procedure for testing that hypothesis is then developed and administered to a number of subjects from a population whose characteristics are known to the researcher. The results are interpreted strictly as verifying or falsifying the theory. With respect to a theory of cognitive development, for example, subjects from several cultures may be tested, not in order to compare them on particular abilities, but in order to assess the generality of the theory. Normally, in theory evaluation there are no in-group tests; the investigator attempts to develop separate hypothesis-testing procedures for the several cultures to be tested.

Piagetian research is often done cross-culturally, and it is often unclear just exactly what is being tested. For example, although on some level all Piagetian research is a test of aspects of Piaget's theory—usually of the universality of a particular

25

stage—cross-cultural tests of Piaget's theory at the same time focus on the testing of subjects and vary in the interpretation of obtained differences between subject groups. Price-Williams (1961), for example, modifies the standard procedure until the between-culture differences are removed. Hence he generally blames obtained differences on the task. Greenfield (1966), on the other hand, accepts her results as, for example, indicating nonconservation in Wolof children. Here differences are attributed to the children and confidence is placed in the task. These choices are also tied up with an implicit view of Piagetian theory, and so the issues are not simple. Price-Williams, having eliminated differences, can say that he has validated Piagetian theory, at least the universality of conservation. Greenfield could argue that she has provided evidence that the theory is wrong and that culturally variable conditions affect such abilities as conservation.

The present study is not any more pure a case than those by Price-Williams and Greenfield. But it reverses the order of these priorities, so that the testing of theory is the main goal and subject ability is measured only in order to permit the testing of theory. As it happens, however, if all of the stages did not appear, it would be quite impossible to ask how they are organized in development.

Development of Test

From earlier research done by our group, we had learned that Eskimo chidlren could solve problems that apparently required operational thinking. Moreover, the Eskimo children were found to be comfortable with test situations, provided that the materials were figural, and provided also that they could respond motorically rather than verbally. Unfortunately, the preliminary test battery had included different types of tests for different stages, and so efforts to extract evidence for the presence of a developmental hierarchy of abilities were frustrated.

The preliminary studies done by our group were efforts

to translate Piaget's descriptions of the quality of thought characteristic of each of the stages into tests that would not be too uncomfortable for Eskimo subjects. Some of these tests simply adapted Piagetian procedures to the extent that: (1) test environments were created in which the materials were familiar; (2) the experimenter did not have to give any complex verbal instructions; and (3) the subjects did not have to talk. One test went even further. It represents an effort to define aspects of concrete operations in terms of a stimulus configuration not unlike that used in an indigenous game.

Although the results are not of any real interest, the tests are. From these several efforts to operationalize aspects of Piagetian theory for testing Eskimo children, a great deal was learned, especially about characterizing the attributes central to each stage and the problems involved in designing instruments to measure them.

In the first of the four preliminary tests, the materials consisted of a set of wooden blocks having one each of two sizes (large and small), of three shapes (circle, triangle, square) and of four colors (red, blue, yellow, green). After being trained to a specific level of familiarity with the three experimentally relevant dimensions of size, shape, and color, the subjects were presented with a series of test items. Each test item consisted of three pairs of blocks plus a single block. Each pair of blocks was an example of a rule, such as "pairs of blocks must be the same shape and color, with size being irrelevant"; the single block could be paired with one but not the other of two *binary-choice* blocks to form a fourth example of the rule. For some items, there was no correct choice, only a more and a less correct choice. Subjects were asked to indicate which of the binary-choice pair of blocks should be paired with the single block.

The test is of interest because it assesses: (1) the ability to infer a relationship from examples of that relationship; (2) the ability to construct another example of a relationship that is known; (3) the ability to evaluate and to compare objects in terms of their component dimensions; and (4) the ability to

27

The Development of Adaptive Intelligence

select a most appropriate object or response when the best object for responding is not available.

When we analyzed the results of this test, it became apparent that the difficulty of the relationships to be inferred was a function of the nature, as well as of the number, of the dimensions participating in the relationship. That is, subjects were able to infer most easily relationships involving shape; color relationships were somewhat more difficult; and size relationships were much more difficult than either shape relationships or color relationships. Of much greater significance were the discoveries that Eskimo children are very comfortable working with blocks when they can respond motorically by placing a block in an array, and that they quickly realize that the pairs of blocks illustrate relations which they must infer. Because shape and color were found to be salient to Eskimo children, these dimensions were used in designing the new test, in which the measures of operational thinking all involve the use of color and shape information.

The second of the four early tests involved an apparatus consisting of a panel with up to four two-position switches mounted on the front. When each switch was appropriately set, the pushing of a button on the front of the panel would close a circuit and turn on a small light, also on the front of the panel. Subjects were shown how the switches and the button worked and were encouraged to try all the possible combinations of switch settings, for one and then for two switches, in attempting to turn on the light. Test items consisted of a series of problems with three or four switches to be set in every possible way, in order to determine the ways that would permit the lighting of the light. (There are eight different ways, or patterns, in which three switches could be set, and sixteen different patterns in which four switches can be set.)

The test assesses: (1) the ability to envision a set of possibilities, and (2) the ability to employ a procedure that facilitates the enumeration or evaluation of each member of a set of possibilities, without repetition. The main dependent variable was the number of omitted possibilities and redundancies in the three

28

switch problems. The results of this test were also scored for the extent to which a sequence of settings indicated a systematic search strategy.

This test was helpful in developing measures for the ability to enumerate all possible combinations. The analysis of results was useful in that we encountered some irregularities of performance which made it obvious that limitations of memory may seriously contaminate measures of the ability to envision a set of possibilities. Thus, every part of the new test was designed so that subjects have external referents for things they wish to recall.

The third early test was administered using several pairs of rectangular boards made of clear plexiglass. Some of these boards were marked with colored arrows that permitted the identification of four unique positions. Subjects were thoroughly familiarized with the four positions or orientations that a board might assume, and with the three permissible transformations or disorientations that could be used to change the orientation of a board. A transformation consisted of a 180° rotation of a board about one of three well-defined axes. The three permissible transformations, taken together with the transformation called *no transformation,* form a four-group not unlike the INRC group. If one position or orientation of the board is thought of as representing the statement (p.q), with p indicating the direction of the colored arrow and q the color of those arrows, then the three permissible transformations of the board will yield, respectively, the statements $(\bar{p}.q)$, $(p.\bar{q})$, and $(\bar{p}.\bar{q})$, because the transformations in question change either the directionality of the arrows, the color of the arrows, or both. The subjects were presented with tasks such as: specifying the final orientation of a board, given the initial orientation and one or more transformations; indicating what transformation would result in a given orientation of the board; and obtaining a specified final orientation of the board in more than one way, given an initial orientation of the board.

The board test has two interesting features. First, this

test defines operations on skills known to be overlearned in the culture of the subjects tested. Eskimo children in some villages on the North Slope (notably Wainwright) play a game in which one child draws a house floor plan in the sand for another child who must try to guess which house in the village is being represented. The boards used in the test were marked with taped on lines which, except for their symmetrical configuration, approximated the sand drawings of floor plans with respect to size, shape, and complexity. In some truly non-Western cultures, the patterns and abilities involved in games, weaving, and so forth may be the only possible bases for developing tests of operational thinking, because it is important that tests of operational thinking build on skills that are known to be overlearned in the cultures in which those tests are to be administered. It may be possible to insure that overlearning is established, so that lack of familiarity with the structure to be operated on can be ruled out as a possible explanation for failure in the performance of an operational task. Second, the test materials permit the establishment of a perceptual mapping of logical statements and a motoric mapping of logical operations.

The fourth early test, designated the *formal* test, was intended to be a test of formal operations. The materials for this test were wooden cubes, which were either black or white, and wooden diamonds, which were red, blue, green, or yellow. The formal test, too, represents a mapping of a propositional calculus into a set of test materials. Statements were represented by two wooden cubes. The first cube indicated "p, q" if white, and "$\bar{p}, \bar{q}$" if black; the second cube indicated "and" if white, and "or" if black, so that, for example, a black cube and a white cube represented that statement $\bar{p}.\bar{q}$. The wooden diamonds represented operations similar to the four logical operations of the formal stage: identity, reciprocal, correlative, and negation, with each of the four operations represented by a different color. The test was presented simply as a game with blocks, and logical terminology was not employed. Tasks included: indicating what proposition would result from the performance of a given operation on a given proposition; indicating what operator would relate two given propositions; and indicating what single operator would have the same effect as two operators applied sequentially. The upper levels of the test involved only operators, with one task being that of indicating which one operator could replace a set of three operators. These upper-level tasks were thought of as involving the ability to perform operations upon operations.

The formal test shares some limitations of the board test with respect to the number of different kinds of statements that may be mapped into the test materials, even though these two tests differ with respect to the manner in which operations are represented—namely, with physical transformation of a board in the case of the board test and with blocks of different colors in the case of the formal test. Very few subjects were able successfully to solve the more complicated portions of the formal test. And it was obvious that subjects were not able to perform above chance level when operators were presented in an abstract and detached way, without a representation of their effect on more concrete materials.

The formal test and the board test, although each presented difficulties, provided experience in the mapping of logical statements and operations into testing materials. It should be obvious, on the basis of these two different mappings, that logical relations, once abstracted, can be mapped in many different formally equivalent ways across a wide variety of stimulus materials.

In summarizing the results of the four early tests, it is important to mention that, in general, all four tests correlate significantly with age, indicating the appropriateness of the tests for the subject sample (colored blocks, $r = .549$; machine, $r = .281$; board, $r = .666$; formal, $r = .264$; $N = 72$). With the exception of the scores on the machine test, which approached significance, all of the tests correlated significantly with the WISC Block Design Test, indicating that the other three tests assess basic cognitive abilities (colored blocks, $r = .543$; machine, $r = -.234$; board, $r = .679$; formal, $r = .336$; $N = 72$).

3

The Eskimo Sample

To develop a viable design for the present research project, given its focus on demonstrating cross-cultural invariance in cognitive development, one needs an accurate understanding of the tested culture. This understanding is necessary because, in order to identify a population as suitable for testing the theory, one must be able to place confidence in that population—in this case Eskimos in general and the Point Hope sample in particular—as normal members of a successful human culture. Moreover, an understanding of the culture is needed if one is to develop a test procedure and test materials that are appropriate for the tested population. The ethnography below provides evidence for a highly evolved cultural adaptation and locates the sample as a relatively pure and stable group of North Slope Eskimos.

The Eskimo Sample

Eskimo Culture

If *intelligence* refers to a characteristic of the species that is adaptive in the Piagetian sense, then North Slope coastal Eskimos are a subject population particularly well suited to this perspective. The population would not be extant today had it not evolved an adaptive intelligence. The circumstances of life on the North Slope are harsh. The environment of these hunters of large sea mammals is extremely variable, and a great deal of contingency planning and cooperative effort seem to be necessary to maintain the well-being of the group. Eskimo environment contrasts sharply with that of traditional farming groups. In farming cultures, survival is apparently best assured by work which may be hard but which is predictable. There is a right way and a right time to plant and harvest crops, and these rather specific injunctions are handed down from father to son. In contrast, the training Eskimo children receive relevant to the hunting culture seems to consist of the presentation of general principles, which the children must learn to apply in different situations.

The North Slope area is the area from Point Hope north and east along the coast to Barrow and Barter Island and inland to the northern side of the Brooks Range. It is characterized by extreme seasonal variations in temperature. The temperatures in coastal areas of the North Slope occasionally reach 60° F in the summer and usually remain well below 0° F in the winter. Although the coastal temperature is moderated by the sea, there are frequently thirty mile-per-hour winds that intensify the frigid conditions. A more remarkable source of seasonal variation lies in the number of daylight hours. For the three summer months the area receives twenty-four hours of daylight, with the sun dipping toward, but never below, the horizon. During the spring and again during the fall the area experiences three months of days and nights as we know them. During the winter quarter the sun never rises above the horizon, although there are four hours or so a day of grey light.

The Development of Adaptive Intelligence

The ground is frozen solid all year long, except for the top few inches that thaw in the summer. The summer thaw creates on the tundra swampy lakes which make walking and the use of sleds difficult. Because of its small annual precipitation, the area would look like a desert if surface water did not seep into the frozen ground. However, the tundra is covered with flowers, mosses, and lichens in the summer. Further seasonal variation is created by the annual cycle of migrations of animals and the associated annual cycle of hunting activities. This cycle is described in great detail by Milan (1958) and VanStone (1962). Fishing, sealing, walrus and whale hunting, and duck and caribou hunting are all still essential in the economy and social life of the villagers and in their diet.

Circumpolar Eskimos have a highly specialized meat and fat diet. The bulk of the diet of coastal Eskimos is supplied by large sea mammals, although increasingly this has been supplemented with imported foods, such as bread, cereal, eggs, candy, canned goods (especially fruit, fruit juice, and milk), and some meats. Vegetables are still a very minor portion of the diet.

The present population of the North Slope is estimated to consist of five thousand Eskimos and a few scattered white schoolteachers, ministers, and occasional researchers. The Eskimos of the North Slope are distributed in five main villages. Four of the villages—Point Hope, Wainwright, Barrow, and Barter Island —are on the coast; only one village settlement, Anaktuvik Pass, is inland. This settlement is the most recently formed of the villages, and the residents are formerly scattered inland families who only recently came together around a trading post to form a village.

The current distribution of inland and coastal settlements reflects a relatively recent shift in population. There is abundant evidence for a highly specialized adaptation on the North Slope going back at least as far as the seventeenth century—an adaptation which produced two distinct Eskimo groups. The inland group, who lived along two rivers and were primarily hunters of caribou, are called Nunatarmiut (or Nunamiut). The coastal group, who have been primarily hunters of large sea mammals, are called Tareormiut, or Tariemiut (Rainey, 1947). Indeed, the Eskimos themselves make this distinction.

However, since about 1860, when it is thought that the inland group was the more populous of the two, there has been a steady decrease in the number of inland Eskimos, while the coastal population has apparently remained stable. The factor that appears most relevant to the decline in numbers of inland Eskimos is migration to the coastal villages. Spencer (1959) attributes the migration primarily to the loss of economic viability of the inland way of life. That change was brought about by the direct importation of Western goods to the coast by whaling vessels. Inland Eskimos depended on regular trading meetings with coastal Eskimos for many essentials, like oil, but had little more than caribou skins and berries to offer in exchange. It is thought that the bargaining power of the inland Eskimos was increased by the entrepreneurial role that they filled, by obtaining Western goods further south and then selling those goods to the more isolated coastal Eskimos. Hence, Western goods were known in Point Hope as early as the beginning of the eighteenth century, even though the first visit by a European was not until 1926 (VanStone, 1962). By 1880, a great many whaling vessels, attracted by the high price of baleen, brought goods directly to the coast; the direct importation of these goods made it impossible for the inland Eskimos to obtain all their survival needs by trading with the coastal Eskimos. In addition, the increased contact with outsiders—which began about 1850, peaked in about 1880, and continued until the turn of the century—also caused a number of very serious and well-documented epidemics of smallpox, measles, and tuberculosis. In several of these epidemics, the dead were reckoned in thousands, and it appears that a number of large inland groups visiting the coast may have been decimated by the worst epidemics. The coastal population was also severely reduced, some think by as much as half.

All the Eskimos living in circumpolar regions—Alaskan, Canadian, and Greenlandic—speak a language called *Inupiat*.

The Development of Adaptive Intelligence

Spencer (1959, p. 40), describing the language, says, "There is a high degree of inflection, both of nouns and verbs, the principal constructions involving root suffixation. Nouns and verbs offer a tremendous number of possible inflections with numerous noun cases, as well as complex verb constructions, involving mode, tense, negation, validity, and the like." This no doubt accurate description is perhaps a less vivid account of the strangeness of the language than is provided by the following translations (Spencer, 1959, p. 175): Uvanni—here; Aalakesaaktuna —he looks here; keevekesaaktuga—he looks there; piluwiyakteruuvlu—he has a lump on his neck; kanusik keyaksakimna—I wonder what kind of person he is.

Apparently there are lexical variations even among the Alaskan villages, as well as differences in speed and style of speaking. However, the grammar and the basic vocabulary are essentially the same. There is abundant evidence of elaborate visiting and trade agreements between adjacent groups of Eskimos, and it may be speculated that this visiting between adjacent regions has contributed to the homogeneity of the language. There is, however, no record of Greenlandic Eskimos having communicated directly with Alaskan Eskimos in modern history, and so the uniformity of the language is truly remarkable.

South of the Brooks Range, only a few hundred miles away but in an entirely different ecological setting, are the far more numerous Yupik-speaking Eskimos. Although Yupik and Inupiat are considered members of the same Eskimoan language family, they are not mutually comprehensible. It is remarkable that the language and culture of the widely dispersed Inupiat-speaking Eskimos should be so similar, and that the Inupiat and Yupik speakers in Alaska should be so linguistically and culturally divergent.

Point Hope, with a population of about 260, is located 125 miles north of the Arctic Circle on a spit of land projecting into the Arctic Ocean from the northwest coast of Alaska. It is the oldest continually occupied area on the North Slope. Rainey, in 1947, dated an ancient site near the present village as well before A.D. 1000; this earlier and apparently related culture is thought to have had an Asiatic origin. Moreover, although the people of Point Hope have periodically resettled in new locations, it is thought that the members of the present population have been interrelated for at least several hundred years. In this respect, Point Hope differs from other North Slope villages (for example, Wainwright), which have received many of the inland Eskimos who have recently migrated to the coast. The stability of the Point Hope population and the location of the village may help to account for the preservation of the traditional hunting way of life and its concomitant social forms, despite the villagers' adoption of some of the conveniences of the modern world.

A century ago, dog sleds and skin boats were the only available means of transportation. Nonetheless, the Eskimos of Point Hope frequently took long trips to regular fishing and sealing camps, as well as to other Eskimo villages where they traded their goods. The use of more modern transportation systems on the North Slope has been frustrated by the terrain. Roads and railroads, for example, are difficult or impossible to build and maintain because of problems created by the permafrost. Thus, land travel is limited to dog sleds and snowmobiles. And for long trips, snowmobiles are considered unreliable.

The most important and the earliest means of access to the North Slope from the nonarctic world was, and continues to be, via the sea. However, travel by sea is limited to a very short period in August, when the ice pack moves far enough from shore to permit the safe passage of boats from the south. Once a year a supply boat, the North Star, owned by the Bureau of Indian Affairs (BIA), brings up the year's supplies for the villagers and the village stores. All major goods—oil, food staples, building materials—must be anticipated a year in advance. The North Star comes up in August as the ice pack is receding and then races up the coast, stopping at each village, where everyone helps to unload so that the boat can make the round trip before the ice pack returns to shore in late August. Some years the ship does not make it to some of the villages, and other complex and

37

costly arrangements have to be made. Access to the outside world has increased enormously in the past twenty years, with the establishment of airstrips in the villages. There are now regular mail planes and, in some cases, regular commercial flights, as well as charter flights. Point Hope now has three regular commercial flights a week to Kotzebue, 175 miles south, from which point one can fly to Fairbanks and out.

Increased contact with the nonarctic world in the past 150 years has dramatically affected some forms of Eskimo life, while other forms have remained amazingly stable. Many Eskimos now have jobs in the post office, as teachers' aides, janitors, at the Distant Early Warning Line sites, in the native store, and so on; others receive welfare. The money from these jobs, however, is used primarily for the purchase of imported items such as clothing, ammunition, washing machines, radios, and supplementary goods, rather than for staples. In order to survive, the Eskimos must still obtain food from the immediate environment. Everything is so expensive on the North Slope that, if the Eskimos had to depend entirely on cash for their food, they would be forced to give up many if not all of the basic modern amenities that they currently enjoy.

The persistence of whaling and walrus hunting in the villages contributes to the perpetuation of many important social forms. The large size of the game makes it inevitable that food gathering and distribution are group activities. Traditional obligations were primarily to relatives and hunting partners, and extensive sharing among these groups is still much in evidence today. Eskimos continue to hunt polar bear and caribou and several smaller animals, including varieties of fox. At certain times of the year many people fish, and in Point Hope virtually everyone goes duck hunting in early summer when thousands of ducks pass over a nearby lagoon in their annual migration. But in the coastal economy, these smaller food sources have never figured as prominently as the large sea mammals. The particular adaptation of circumpolar Eskimos has indeed been attributed to the central importance in their lives of whale hunting and its attendant cultural forms.

Although many, indeed most, of the specific rituals (Spencer, 1959) appear to have disappeared from common practice in recent years, the general form of main celebrations as well as the basic activities that typified them have been preserved. The spring whaling festival with its traditional pattern of food distribution, the summer foot races, and the occasional village feast and dance with traditional drums and songs are still much in evidence.

Virtually all ethnographies of North Slope Eskimos, beginning with that of the earliest expedition (Commander Ray's visit to Point Barrow in 1885), comment on the friendliness, sweet nature, dignity, and helpfulness of the Eskimos. Adult Eskimos expect each other to work hard, to be honest and self-reliant, and to control aggressive impulses. Although there is an emphasis on doing one's best, and the playing of competitive games persists as a common village social activity, no one is ever supposed to stand out too much or to embarrass anyone else. Those who are unable to look after themselves in spite of their best efforts are neither made fun of nor permitted by the community to go hungry.

The child-rearing patterns that have produced this behavior do not appear to have changed very much in the last century. Children are raised with great love and affection and a minimum of rules. Most of the rules involve survival: not playing in the ocean, wearing one's parka, and so on. Weaning is a very gentle and gradual process, and infants are utterly indulged by both parents for their first two or three years. Until they are four or five years old, children rarely go out to play, except perhaps in front of the house, and they are kept with the mother or some other female relative. Although they are expected to be obedient to their parents, no real work is expected of Eskimo children until they are about ten or eleven years old; and even then they are only expected to help with light chores or with activities thought to be important for their education. Childhood is remembered by adults as a time of great warmth and happiness (Lantis, 1960).

Indeed, the Eskimo method of child-rearing is clearly suited for producing self-directed but socially responsible adults. Eskimo children are extremely obedient and do not fight. A child who does something wrong is rarely punished unless his behavior was antisocial. Physical punishment is very rare, and even verbal scolding is not common. When a child is out playing he lives in a world of children, and he clearly has a life of his own in which he is the comfortable master of an ever-widening circle around the village. The adult theory is in fact very Piagetian. They see a child's growth as essentially self-motivated, and they feel that when a child is ready, he will learn.

The members of our research team observed that Eskimo children do an extraordinary amount of intent watching; whenever an adult is engaged in an interesting activity, there is a cluster of children around him. Once, when a child happened to be watching him, a member of our team performed a complex procedure, putting measured quantities of chemicals into a series of test tubes. Then he asked the interested child what he had done. The child repeated the procedure perfectly. We have found Eskimo children particularly attentive in other ways as well. They are very quick to catch on to unfamiliar ideas and procedures.

One aspect of Eskimo life that has been introduced entirely by outside influences is formal education. The missionaries to Alaska have devised an Inupiat dictionary and have taught Eskimos to read and write in their native tongue. However, the presence of missionaries has also led to the dissolution of some important social forms—such as the dances that traditionally celebrated successful whaling expeditions—that the church discouraged in its early years there.

A school was built near Point Hope as early as 1890 by the Episcopalian church, with government help. This school persisted until 1920, and the first government school was begun in 1904. In 1931, the schools were taken over by the Bureau of

The Eskimo Sample

Indian Affairs (VanStone, 1962). Since about 1970, the village councils have had repeated opportunities to decide if they would rather be in the state system. Point Hope opted for the change in 1970. Although there have been one or two native teachers in other villages on the North Slope, these much discussed and admired teachers are the exceptions rather than the rule. Virtually all North Slope schoolteachers have been from the lower forty-eight states.

For their high school education, all North Slope children go to BIA schools further south. Most Point Hope students go to Mount Edgecumbe in Sitka on the south coast of Alaska or to Chemawa in Oregon, but this pattern seems to be changing. Increasing numbers of Barrow children have been in boarding home programs in Fairbanks. And there has been recent progress on plans for a Barrow high school, which might be attended by North Slope children from other villages as well.

Parents place a sufficiently high value on education so that they encourage their children to leave home for a whole academic year to attend these distant schools. Needless to say, the dramatic change in environment and life style and the distance from home make the whole experience very difficult for both parents and children. The increasing pressure by the North Slope Native Association for a high school in northern Alaska may result in a less traumatic schooling arrangement.

The four years that Eskimo adolescents spend at boarding school seem to result in a gradual breakdown of the traditional adult roles, particularly for the boys. Women traditionally learn most complex adult skills, such as the making of walrus-skin boats, after marriage, usually in their twenties. Although the school interruption is probably responsible for the lateness of marriage, the pattern of learning these difficult skills after marriage is an old one. A man however is supposed to have learned to hunt during adolescence; and it may be speculated that today's adolescent males are not as competent as the cultural traditions would predict because they spend so much time away at

41

school. Nonetheless, most boys hunt when they are home and whenever there is an opportunity to go hunting with someone more experienced.

This weakening of traditional forms is more clearly demonstrated by Eskimos who continue their education beyond high school. Until very recently, virtually no Eskimos living on the North Slope had college degrees. Those who attended college, and so were away from the village for at least eight years, lack the traditional hunting skills and are overeducated for the available types of village employment. Thus they are not likely to return to the village after completion of their studies. Some recent high school graduates are being encouraged to attend college and then to return to teach in the village primary schools. Certainly the construction of a high school on the North Slope would result in suitable local employment for college graduates.

In sum, the Point Hope culture is generically and culturally homogeneous and well defined, and it has been both geographically and numerically stable for some time. Moreover, the culture can be seen to be sufficiently distinct from our own to provide an interesting target sample for the testing of invariance.

The fact that children of Point Hope are accustomed to classroom situations and activities suggests that they would not be unduly uncomfortable in, or disturbed by a testing situation. Nonetheless, it is important to know what kinds of test content and test format might introduce difficulties not associated with the cognitive abilities to be tested. In attempting to determine, beforehand, what culturally related factors might confound an attempt to assess cognitive development in Eskimo children, several early studies of Eskimos were reviewed.

Psychological Studies of North Slope Eskimos

Eells (1933) was among the first to administer intelligence tests to native groups in Alaska. His work was part of an educational survey—of schooled Aleut, Indian, and Eskimo children—that was aimed at curriculum improvements. The

42

The Eskimo Sample

Stanford-Binet Intelligence Scale and the Goodenough Draw-a-Man test were administered. The Stanford-Binet was modified to include objects that were familiar in Alaskan daily life. All three groups scored significantly lower than the white standardization norms. Eskimos scored significantly lower than Aleuts and Indians, who scored approximately the same on this test. This difference in scores is explained in terms of inadequacy of sampling rather than of Eskimo inferiority. The relatively poor performance of the Eskimos is interesting in view of their superiority to other native groups on more recent tests (MacArthur, 1968; Vernon, 1969). The Goodenough scale was administered because its nonverbal nature was thought to make it less subject to cultural bias. The order of the scores was the same for the three samples on this test, but all three groups scored higher than they had on the Stanford-Binet. Eells concluded that verbal factors may account for as much as fifteen IQ points in the inferiority of native to Western white samples.

Vernon (1969) administered a battery, including both individual and group tests, to fifty Canadian Eskimo boys, aged ten to twelve years, of the Northwest territories above the Arctic Circle. He attempted to delineate meaningful clusters of abilities as reflected in the test results and to relate performance to environmental factors. The unexpectedly poor performance of both Indians and Eskimos on an arithmetic achievement test was attributed to the use of the highly verbal new math in the schools. On spelling comprehension and usage and group vocabulary tests, the Eskimos were only slightly below average, but their scores on the Terman-Merrill individual vocabulary test were quite low. These results suggested to Vernon that, despite the verbal fluency they exhibited, the Eskimos were handicapped in their ability to think and learn in English. The Eskimos also did well on a set of spatial tests, including Kohs Blocks, picture recognition, and an embedded figures test. This pattern of results seemed to Vernon to support the notion that experience at coping with the physical environment, as well as opportunities to manipulate objects, is involved in spatial abilities.

43

The Development of Adaptive Intelligence

Berry's (1966) interest in the relationship between the cultural and ecological characteristics of a society and its perceptual skills led him to test these perceptual skills in the Eskimos of Baffin Island and in the Temne of Sierra Leone, two groups which differed in several respects relevant to his hypothesis. The Temne enjoy a more varied visual environment than the Eskimos. Moreover their livelihood, obtained by sedentary farming, does not require some of the perceptual skills essential to the survival of the Eskimos, who were nomadic hunters. Cultural differences complement and augment these ecological differences. The Eskimos can express more spatial concepts in their language; their arts, crafts, and map-making are more elaborate than those of the Temne; and they are more permissive in their treatment of children than the Temne, who are very strict and demand conformity.

Because he believed that these factors and their concomitant skill differences would be influenced by the degree of westernization, Berry chose two samples for each group. Ninety subjects were drawn from a traditional community (Pond Inlet, for the Eskimos), and thirty subjects from a transitional community (Frobisher Bay, for the Eskimos). In addition, Berry compared the Eskimo and Temne samples with a Scottish sample, to provide a Western reference group. In accord with the distinction made in the previous two samples, sixty-two Scottish subjects were drawn from a small village and sixty from a city. Subjects ranged in age from ten to more than forty years. Four spatial tests were administered: Kohs Blocks; six of Witkin's Embedded Figures; Morrisby Shapes; and series A, AB, and B of Raven's matrices. Time on all tests was either extended or unlimited. Eskimos scored higher than the Temne on the four standard tests of spatial ability. The more westernized groups scored higher than the more traditional groups. In addition, scores were associated with education level. Berry calls attention to the high intercorrelations among the scores on the four spatial tests, which seem to suggest that they are actually measuring the same skill for

44

these samples that they measure in the West. This, in turn, lends a degree of reliability to the interpretation of the results.

On the whole, the Temne were found to differ vastly from the Eskimos who, in turn, resembled the Scots in their test performance. Graphs of scores across age had similar shapes for Eskimos and Scots. The graphs for the Temne were flatter, suggesting that the skills tested develop less at the appropriate time, because there is little ecological or cultural demand for them. Berry points out that the differences in each case between traditional and transitional samples indicate a cultural rather than a racial explanation for the differences in skills. One of the present authors has found additional evidence of the superior perceptual abilities of the Eskimos. Bock and Feldman's (1969) analysis of test scores on series A through D of Raven's matrices revealed that the generally low overall scores obtained obscured considerable interseries differences. On series B and D, the Eskimo performance compared favorably to that of the Scots in a mining community where the test was normed. The more perceptual series A seemed to depend on ideas of good form that might be culture specific, while series C drew on skill at permutation that might likewise be differentially stressed in different cultures.

An English vocabulary test, given by Bock and Feldman (1969) required subjects to choose one of four words to complete a sentence. Despite low scores relative to American samples, the ability of the Eskimos to communicate in English is high. This suggests that the size of vocabulary and ability to communicate may be distinct.

We administered the Block Design portion of the Wechsler Intelligence Scale for Children (WISC) to sixty-eight Point Hope children. The WISC has two scales, which yield a general verbal score and a performance or nonverbal score. The Block Design subtest is one of the constituent subtests of the performance score. To facilitate comparisons between the norms and the Eskimo scores, the raw Block Design score for each subject was

Table 1.
WISC BLOCK DESIGN TEST RESULTS

Age	$\bar{X}_1$	N_1	$\bar{X}_2$	N_2	SD_2	$SD_2/\sqrt{N_2}$	Z
7	9.8	5	10	200	3	.21	1.0
8	11.4	9	10	200	3	.21	6.6
9	13.1	6	10	200	3	.21	14.6
10	11.2	10	10	200	3	.21	5.7
11	11.7	8	10	200	3	.21	8.0
12	10.5	6	10	200	3	.21	2.4
13	12.0	8	10	200	3	.21	9.4
14–15	12.0	7	10	400	3	.15	13.3
16–19	11.6	11	10	600	3	.11	15.1

converted to a standard score, and a mean standard score for each of the Eskimo age groups was calculated.

In order to compare Eskimo scores with the published norms for each whole year age group, a Z (standard score) statistic was computed, comparing each of the age groups with $Z = (\bar{x} - 10) / 3\sqrt{200}$, where $3/\sqrt{200}$ is the standard error of the mean. The resulting Z values are tested against zero for significance. Table 1 reports these calculations and shows that the Eskimos are significantly superior to the norm in all age groups but one, the youngest, where their performance is virtually equal to that in the norms. For a Z score of 1.96, $p < .05$, and all of the Z scores except that of the seven year old group exceed this value.

With verbal considerations reduced to a minimum, as in the case of intelligence tests such as the Block Design portion of the Wechsler Intelligence Scale for Children, the performance of Eskimo subjects was comparable to that of White subjects.

4

The Test

$\mathbb{A}$n attempt was made to construct a series of tasks that would span the Piagetian stages from preoperational through formal operational, reusing the same familiar materials throughout the test, with only the nature of the task varying according to the stage being assessed. Using the same materials throughout the test is indispensable for gathering evidence for the hierarchical organization of cognitive abilities. When new tasks are administered at each stage, it is difficult to determine whether failure at any level is due to the child's lack of an operational ability or to his nonattendance to relevant stimulus categories in a new test situation. However, when the same stimulus materials and categories occur throughout, failure on tasks at any level is more safely attributed to true operational failure, because the child must attend to those same categories in order to solve lower level problems.

Two very different sets of stimulus materials were used to

create structurally identical versions of the new test. The main version uses colored blocks, materials that are commonly understood in many cultures and have been found to be readily attended to by Eskimo children. The test analogue involves the use as stimuli of pictures of wild animals whose salient characteristics of size (large and small) and habitat (land and sea) are perhaps specific to the North Slope Eskimo culture. The colored blocks were used for all tasks in the test, while the animal analogue was given in a curtailed form to keep the testing session under an hour for each subject. The test description that follows will be based on the colored block version of the test. The animal analogue will be described as an extension of the concepts tested by the Colored Blocks Test to the culture-specific animal stimulus materials.

The Colored Blocks Test was divided into five sections preceded by two training tasks. Each of these sections can be interpreted as testing abilities characteristic of a particular Piagetian stage. Earlier sections of the test deal with the construction of simple classifications according to color and shape, and later sections construct propositions involving sameness or difference of color and shape. The last sections test the child's ability to transform the relations expressed in these propositions.

Description

The stimulus materials consist of colored blocks, approximately one and a half inches in diameter. The set of blocks includes four values of each of two characteristics—color and shape. The four color values are red, green, yellow, and blue; the four shape values are square, circle, diamond, and triangle (sixteen blocks). There is one complete set of blocks for the subject to use in answering and a set for the tester to use in constructing the problems of the training tasks and Sections I and II. For the remainder of the test, the problems are drawn on seven-by-twelve-inch cards, and the subject answers from his set of blocks.

Training Task 1: The Sort. Only twelve blocks are used

49

for the sorting task—two red, two green, and two yellow squares, and two red, two green, and two yellow circles. These blocks are placed before the subject, and he is then asked to sort them into groups, with the number and the content of the groups unrestricted. After a grouping has been completed, the subject is requested to form another, until three trials are completed.

> *First we're going to use some of my blocks. There are a lot of ways that these blocks can go together. They are alike in a lot of different ways. Put them into piles; make as many piles as you want, and put as many blocks as you want in each pile, any way that you think they should go.*

If the subject should fail to produce a *color sort* (blocks grouped according to color) or a *shape sort* (blocks grouped according to shape), the experimenter then provides the beginnings of the kind of sort that the subject has not yet produced, and the subject is asked to complete it. For example, a subject who produces a color sort but not a shape sort is presented with the beginnings of a shape sort and is asked to finish it. This sorting task permits assessment of a subject's natural tendency to attend to both color and shape, and directs his attention to these characteristics of the blocks.

Training Task 2: Cuing into Relevant Dimensions. The second task consists of eight problems, and introduces a set of blocks of four different colors and four different shapes (sixteen blocks). The stimulus set for each problem is a card containing a partially completed matrix of three blocks (see Figure 1, a–h), and the response set is always the collection of sixteen different blocks. Each problem involves choosing from the response set a block that appropriately completes the matrix (makes the color-shape relationships identical in each vertical pair of blocks). For example, a subject presented with a partial matrix of three red squares may select any one of sixteen answer blocks for completing the matrix; but only a red square would be considered correct.

> *Now I'll show you how these (little cards that blocks are*

The Test

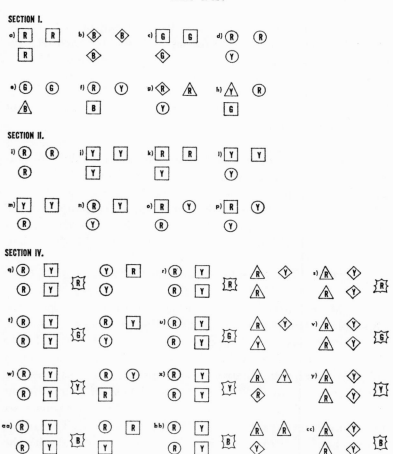

FIGURE 1.
Training Task 2 and Sections I, II, and IV of the
Colored Blocks Test.

placed on) work. *I put down three of my blocks (puts
down three, forming a partial matrix), and you can see
that they go together in a special way. Those (gestures toward subject's blocks) are yours to answer with. Which one
of your blocks goes here? (Point to spot for answer block.)*

51

The Development of Adaptive Intelligence

For the first two problems, two training procedures are available, one for correct responses and one for incorrect responses. Following a correct response, the correct answer block is removed from the response set, and another is requested.

> *That's fine, but if you didn't have this one, which would be the best answer?*

This procedure encourages the subject to select a minimally incorrect response. For the stimulus set consisting of three red squares, such a response would be any red or any square block. The blocks with the value of the dimension in terms of which the subject has just responded are covered, and he is thus encouraged to select a block with the correct value of the remaining dimension.

> *That's fine, but what if you didn't have any red blocks?*

More extensive training follows an incorrect response to either of the first two problems. Following an incorrect response, all of the blocks of the response set are covered, except blocks that have the correct value for, first of all, the dimension of color. For the partial matrix consisting of three red squares, the blocks available to the subject are red blocks of four different shapes. The subject selects blocks from this limited response set until the correct answer is chosen (that is, red square). The correct answer block and the block initially chosen are placed with the matrix. Within this perceptual context, the correct answer is invariably selected by the subject as the best of the two. This procedure is then repeated, with the response set limited to blocks which have the correct value for the dimension of shape (four square blocks of four different colors), which encourages the subject to attend to the color dimension.

Problems 3 to 8 confront the subjects with increasing numbers of differences in the shape and color of the blocks of the stimulus matrix. It is important that the subjects attend to differences of shape and color among the blocks, because all latter manipulations in the test will depend on relationships of this kind. This section simply directs the subject's attention to the color and shape of the blocks. Although it cannot have the effect of making all subjects equally familiar with these characteristics, it at least establishes some set to attend to them.

Section I. The stimulus set and the response set for this section include only red and yellow squares and red and yellow circles. The stimulus arrangement for each of the five problems comprising Section I is identical to the arrangement used in the training problems (see Figure 1, i–m). In questions 1 and 2, all three stimulus blocks are identical. In questions 3 and 4, two of the blocks share a common value of one dimension and have different values of the other. For question 5, two of the blocks differ on both dimensions.

In Section I, the task for the subject is that of choosing an answer block that makes the right-hand vertical pair relationships identical to those in the left-hand pair. The left-hand vertical pair of blocks may be the same or may differ in color or shape or both. To respond correctly, a subject must select an answer block that is both the correct color and the correct shape. However, because the two blocks in the top row are identical in each of the problems in this section, the relationship between the blocks of column 1 can be reproduced merely by choosing the answer block that is identical to the lower block in column 1. Thus, in this first and least complex section of the test, it is possible for a subject to respond correctly simply by perceptual matching.

Section II. Section II of the developmental sequence consists of three problems (see Figure 1, n–p). The stimulus set and the response set are the same as in Section I, and the stimulus arrangement is identical.

As in Section I, the left column of blocks illustrates a particular relationship, and the subject's task is to choose an answer block that will establish a relationship in the second column that is identical to the relationship in the first. In Section II, however, the top two blocks are different, and hence the correct response cannot be obtained simply by selecting an answer block that matches the block in the lower left. In fact, the correct answer may be a block that is not present in the stimulus matrix at all. To solve the problems in this section, a subject must first conceptualize the relation between the left side blocks, and he must then reproduce that same relationship but using different instances. The problems in this section require an ability to abstract general relations between pairs of blocks from particular instances, and these problems should be successfully solved by concrete operational children.

Section IV. This section is presented here because it is given to the subject directly following Section II; however, it is called Section IV because of its predicted position in the developmental sequence.

Section IV consists of four subsections, each of which contains three cards. Each of the four subsections introduces a different logical operation. The four operations involved are symbolized by red, yellow, green, and blue three-quarter-inch cubes. The red cube symbolizes an identity operation in which the color and shape relationships illustrated by the pairs of blocks in the left matrix are reproduced in the right matrix. The yellow operation changes the shape relationship illustrated by the pairs of blocks in the left matrix but does not affect the color relationship. Conversely, the green operation changes the color relationship illustrated by the pairs of blocks in the left matrix, while the shape relationship remains unaffected. The blue operation changes both the color relationship and the shape relationship illustrated by the two pairs of blocks in the left matrix (see Figure 1, q–cc).

The stimulus and response sets for the first problem (see Figure 1, q, t, w, aa) of each subsection are limited to red and yellow circles and squares, as in Sections I and II of the test. The subjects are presented with two matrices, similar to those in Sections I and II. The first matrix is completed and consists of two pairs of identical blocks; the second matrix is partially completed. One of the colored cubes is present between the matrices.

54

The Test

The task is to complete the partial matrix with an answer block, as in Sections I and II.

> *Now we're going to try these big cards (to older subjects: "These are more fun.") I'm going to show you how these work. These two go together (repeat while pointing up and down between the blocks in each of the three completed vertical pairs); which one would go with this one? (Point at top block of incomplete pair).*

The first problem in each subsection is intended to introduce to the subject the concept of an operation. It illustrates how operations work by locating them between two matrices, within the familiar task of completing a matrix. These problems may be solved by considering the color and shape relationships in the right-hand matrix alone. After completing the right matrix, the operator cubes are introduced by the following procedure:

> *Leave that answer for a second because I'm going to show you what the little (red, green, yellow or blue) cube in the middle does. The cube in the middle shows you how all these (gesture to four blocks on left side of cube) go with all these (gesture to four blocks on right side of cube), how these two (point to first vertical pair of left matrix) go with these two (point to first pair of right matrix), and how these two (point to second pair of left matrix) go with these two (point to second pair of right matrix). Can you see what the red cube does?*

The procedure and the format for the second problem in each subsection are the same as for the first problem, but the materials are different. For the second problem, the right-hand blocks, as well as the response set, consist of red and yellow diamonds and triangles, while the left-hand blocks are red and yellow squares and circles (see Figure 1, r). The second problem in each subsection indicates to the subject that the same operation

55

can be applied to new and different stimuli and hence should facilitate his realizing that it is the relationship illustrated by the pairs of blocks in a matrix, and not the specific colors and shapes of those blocks, that is affected by the presence of the various operators.

The stimulus set for the third problem in each of the four subsections consists of red and yellow diamonds and triangles; and the response set consists of red and yellow squares and circles. The subject is presented with a left matrix in which the two blocks in each vertical pair are identical, followed by an operator cube. His task is to generate a matrix on the right which illustrates the relationship that results when the operator cube is applied to the relationship illustrated by the pairs of blocks in the left matrix (Figure 1, s).

> *Now if you start with these (gesture to matrix on left side of cube), and you have a red (or green or yellow or blue) cube in the middle (point to cube), what would you have over here? (Gesture to right side of cube).*

In formulating a response, the subject is permitted to look back at the preceding card (problem 2); however, problem 2 is hidden when the subject is actually responding. This procedure was adopted to reduce the extent to which memory is involved in attempting to solve the third problem.

The first two problems in each of the four subsections of this section introduce to the subjects the notion of an operation, and emphasize the effect of operations on the relationship between blocks, not the specific color or shape of particular blocks. In the third problem of Section IV, the child has to apply the operations to the left-hand matrix in order to produce a right-hand matrix.

An additional section of the test, referred to as *Mixed Inputs,* was not used as a part of the developmental sequence. Although it was administered late in the sequence (following Section III), this section is described here because the materials and format are identical to those in Section IV. The Mixed Inputs section consists of two subsections, each with three problems. The operation performed in the first subsection is red (identity); in the second subsection, it is the yellow (shape) operation. This section evaluates the ability of a subject to perform an operation on a relationship, as in Section IV. For this section, however, the subject must operate on a relationship in which the two blocks that make up each vertical pair are not identical, but have different values for at least one of the two dimensions, shape and color (see Figure 2).

Subjects who pass Section IV at the formal level do so by having the ability to apply their formal operations to all possible input sets. They realize that the input set characterized as *same color–same shape* is only one of several possible input sets, in the sense that their operations are sufficiently abstract that they apply with no modification to other possible input sets like the same color, different shape stimuli used in the Mixed Input questions. The only difference between the operations involved in Section IV and the Mixed Input questions lies in the more generalized input set of the Mixed Input questions. Piaget's formal model characterizes the abilities measured by both sections as aspects of the same underlying structure.

Section III. In Section III, a chart is introduced to eliminate the need to remember what the cubes do (see Figure 3). The chart contains four pairs of matrices, each pair associated with an operator cube; within each matrix there are four vertical pairs of blocks. The stimulus set for each problem consists of a card depicting two completed matrices, similar to those in Sections I and II of the test. The subject's task is to choose the operator cube that symbolizes the left to right relationship between matrices in any one pair. There is one problem of this kind for each of the four operations.

> *These two go together (repeat four times, pointing to each of the four vertical pairs of blocks). Which one of these cubes (gesture to the four colored cubes) would you put here (point to answer space) to make all these (gesture to right side of card) go with all these (gesture to left side*

57

The Development of Adaptive Intelligence

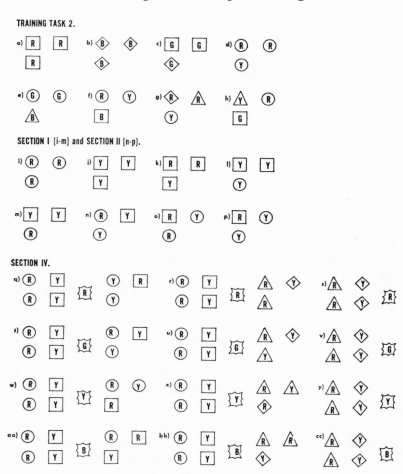

FIGURE 2.

Sections III, V, and Mixed Inputs of the Colored Blocks Test.

of card), *to make these two go with these two (point to the first pair on each side), and these two go with these two? (Point to second pair on each side.)*

The subject is encouraged to refer to the chart in choosing the appropriate operator for each problem.

58

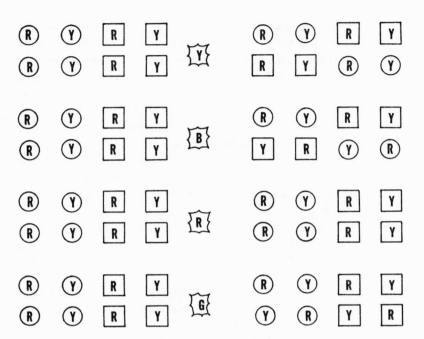

FIGURE 3. The chart.

For this question, you can use this chart (gesture to the chart). You can see that these two go together (repeat for each vertical pair on left side of red cube). This chart shows you what happens to these pairs when you use red (gesture to right side of red cube). This line (gesture to right side of green cube) shows you what happens to these pairs (point to the vertical pairs on the left side of the green cube) when you use green. (Similar instructions are given for the yellow and blue cubes.) You can find these pairs (point to vertical pairs on left side of operator cube on the problem card) on this side (point to left side of chart) and these pairs (point to vertical pairs on right side of operator cube on the problem card) on this side (point to right side of chart). Now do you see how this chart works? You can use this to answer these questions, it will remind you what the red, green, yellow and blue cubes do,

59

The Development of Adaptive Intelligence

Having four vertical pairs of blocks in each matrix on the chart and two on the problem cards discourages simple matching of the matrices in selecting a response. This reduces the possibility of preoperational children successfully solving these questions.

Section V. Section V consists of a training sequence (Figure 2, g–i) followed by three test questions (Figure 2, k–m). The training sequence consists of two sections, each of which contains two questions. The first question of each section (g and i) introduces to the subjects the notion of the simultaneous use of two operators (for example, red and blue) within the familiar context of completing a matrix. It is structurally similar to the first card for each subsection of Section IV.

The second question of each training section (h and j) uses the completed card as a stimulus. The experimenter explains to the subject the notion of using two operations simultaneously:

> *(Gesturing to the chart) You've seen what the red cube does, and you've seen what the blue cube does. This card shows you what happens when you use the red cube and the blue cube together. Together they make all these (point to left side of card) go with all these (point to right side of card), and they make these two (gesture to first vertical pair of left matrix), go together differently than these two (gesture to first vertical pair of right matrix) and they make these two (gesture to second vertical pair of left matrix) go together differently than these two (gesture to second vertical pair of right matrix).*

The child is asked to figure out which one of the four operators has the same effect as is produced by the two operators in the stimulus.

> *Which one of these cubes (pick up each of the four operator cubes) by itself does the same thing that these two do together?*

The subject is encouraged to use the chart introduced in

The Test

Section III in selecting the appropriate cube. The first training section presents the red and blue operators together (Figure 2, g and h). The effect of the two operators together is to change both the color relationship and the shape relationship illustrated by the vertical pairs of blocks in the left matrix. The blue cube alone has the same effect.

The second training section presents the green and yellow operators together (Figure 2, i and j). These operations also change both the color relationship and the shape relationship illustrated by the pairs of blocks in the left matrix. The answer is again the blue cube.

The main part of Section V consists of three problems (Figure 2, k–m). Both the stimulus set and the response set consist of four colored cubes. For each problem, the subject is presented with two operator cubes, without input or output matrices, and his task is to select from the complete set of four the one operator cube that has the same effect as the two stimulus cubes. The subject is encouraged to consult the chart previously mentioned in selecting the appropriate cube.

> *You've seen what the red cube does and what the green cube does (gesture to chart). Now, by just using the chart, see if you can show me which cube by itself does the same thing that these two do together.*

Three combinations of cubes are used: (a) red and blue, (b) red and yellow, and (c) yellow and green. Section V is intended to elicit the subject's perception of the group properties of the operations. Successful performance of this task would at least require thinking at a formal operational level, and might involve other abilities as well.

Analogue Task

In addition to the Colored Blocks Test, there is a test which is a cultural analogue to Sections I, II, and IV of the blocks test. The stimulus materials are drawings of arctic animals,

61

approximately two inches square. The entire stimulus set consists of two values for each of two dimensions. The two dimensions are the actual (rather than drawn) size of the animals and their natural habitats. The two values of size are large and small, and the two values of natural habitat are land and sea. The large sea animals were walruses; the small sea animals were seals. The large land animals were bears; and the small land animals were foxes. Whales and fishes were used as the generalization stimuli for large sea and small sea animals on the second question in each of the four series in Section IV.

The first analogue section is structurally identical to Section I of the Colored Blocks Test. The stimulus and response sets consist of drawings of walruses, seals, bears, and foxes. As in Section I of the Colored Blocks Test, the subject is presented with a partial matrix. The task is to complete the matrix with a drawing from the response set.

Section II of the analogue is structurally identical to Section II of the Colored Blocks Test. The stimulus set and response set are the same as in Section I of the analogue. As in Section II of the Colored Blocks Test, the subject must first conceive the relationship between the animals of the first vertical pair in abstract, structural terms, and must then reproduce that relationship with different concrete objects.

The last section of the analogue is structurally identical to Section IV of the Colored Blocks Test. There are four subsections, each with three problems. Each of the subsections introduces one of the four operations. The stimulus materials for the first problem of each subsection consist of walruses, foxes, seals, and bears, and an operator cube. As in the Colored Blocks Test, the subject is presented with two matrices, one completed and one partially completed. One of the colored cubes is present between the matrices. The subject is asked to complete the partial matrix. The left matrix and the operator cube are not part of the task. The experimenter then explains the nature of the operator cube to the subject, by asking him to inspect the relationships illustrated. (See the description of the Colored Blocks Test for procedure.)

The stimulus set for the second problem of each subsection consists of walruses, seals, bears, and foxes. The response set consists of whales, fish, bears, and foxes. The stimulus materials are arranged in two matrices, and the task is to complete the partial matrix. The second problem of each subsection in the Colored Blocks Test served to introduce the notion that the operations can be generalized to new stimuli. (See the description of Section IV of the blocks test.) To introduce this notion, it is necessary that each matrix of a pair contain two values of a dimension that are different from the two values for that dimension in the other matrix. For the second problem of each analogue subsection, the same values—land/sea and large/small— were used in both matrices, but these values were exemplified by different animals. Unlike in the blocks test however the child did not have a completely different stimulus set, but one that was only partially different. With these limitations, the third problem in each subsection is analogous to the third problem in each subsection of the blocks test.

The analogue measures the same abilities as Sections I, II, and IV of the Colored Blocks Test but asks the subject to exercise those abilities on more familiar or salient stimuli. Thus, the test construction and procedure for the Colored Blocks Test and for the analogue are virtually identical. It is obvious that analogues to Sections III and V of the Colored Blocks Test could have been created with the culturally familiar stimulus materials; however, their inclusion would have created an unmanageable increase in testing time. The analogue sections were presented to the subjects immediately before Section I or immediately after Section IV of the Colored Blocks Test. The number of subjects who were presented with the analogue before the corresponding blocks test sections was equal to the number who received the Colored Blocks Test first. The order of presentation did not significantly affect subject performance on either the Colored Blocks Test or the analogue sections, except that performance on the items in Section II of the analogue improved slightly when the Colored Blocks Test was given first.

Giving Test to All Ages

It is one of the central assumptions of this research that an adequate validation of the hierarchical nature of cognitive development must take the form of administering a single test to children of all ages. It is obvious, however, that such an undertaking would run into enormous practical problems if the younger children were totally frustrated by those sections of the test designed to tap abilities beyond their grasp.

The Colored Blocks Test overcomes these practical considerations by allowing for alternative strategies. Thus, in Section II, a preoperational child can continue to respond as he did in Section I. He will be content to do so, but his answer will be incorrect. It should be noted that it is also possible to answer each section correctly with a higher level strategy. For example, Section I can be answered concretely by copying the relationship in the left pair as is required in Section II. Section I can also be answered at a formal level by applying the identity operation to the relationships of the left-hand pair. It is unlikely that any subject would use such advanced strategies in the earlier sections, because there would be no signal or task-constraint to do so. In the absence of such cues, the use of higher order processes would be highly inefficient. The important point, however, is that the use of processes at a more advanced level would yield the correct response. On the other hand, the use of lower level processes produces incorrect responses, except in two instances (discussed below) where an elaborate and highly unlikely lower level strategy could possibly be used to produce a correct response. Because of this test structure, no child is ever credited with the abilities of a stage beyond his present capacities, yet all children can answer all of the questions.

The two possible exceptions to this feature of the test structure involve Sections III and IV. First, the questions of Section III can be solved preoperationally if the subject matches the stimulus pairs to identical pairs on the chart. However, as previously mentioned, the matrices of this chart each contain four pairs of blocks, while the stimulus matrices contain only two pairs. This makes matching unlikely. Furthermore, the evidence presented in Chapter Five demonstrates that the ability to perform correctly on Section III tasks appears with the ability to solve the Section II (concrete) tasks and not the Section I (preoperational) tasks. Second, although Section IV is conceived as a test of formal abilities, it is possible to solve it correctly at the concrete level. At the concrete level, the child can merely construct a matrix which has the same color-shape relationship as the right-hand sides of the training cards he has just seen. Alternatively, at the formal level, the child can actually perform the appropriate operation on the relationships of the left-hand side. It is impossible to state definitely which strategy was used, because the children were never able to describe how they did it. However, there is reason to believe, on the basis of the evidence presented in Chapter Five (that Section IV taps a later stage than Sections II and III) that the formal approach was used by the majority of the children who succeeded at the task.

5

The Results

The Colored Blocks Test was administered to sixty-seven North Slope Eskimos during the summer of 1971. This test was designed to investigate the congruence of the performance of Eskimo children and adolescents with one of Piaget's basic hypotheses: that cognitive development is hierarchical—that it follows a logically invariant sequence of staged abilities. For this purpose five cognitive operations were defined: (a) completing a matrix by attending to one set of relations between attributes (Section I of the test); (b) completing a matrix by coordinating two sets of relations between attributes (Section II); (c) identifying the operation performed on a set of relations between attributes (Section III); (d) operating on a set of relations between attributes (Section IV); and (e) operating on operations (Section V).

For the purpose of experimental investigation, two aspects of Piaget's developmental hypothesis were operationalized: sequence and stage. The rationale for the analysis follows.

66

The Results

Model Behind the Analysis

Operations, Tasks, and Psychological States: Sequencing Hypothesis. The behavioral characteristics in which we are mainly interested express the capacity to perform specific tasks that involve a unique set of logical operations. In fact, the tasks are such that a hierarchic structure of logical operations can be identified with the tasks. In this case, the most complex task—that is, the double cube items—includes the less complex operations used to complete the other tasks.

The logical operations required to solve the tasks can be arranged in a sequence of complexity. This sequence also represents a hierarchic arrangement, because each subsequent operation entails, in part, prior operations.

The major psychological issue to which the above logical structure of operations is relevant is the hypothesis that the development of cognitive ability—that is, changes in ability with age—is postulated to be in exactly the same sequence. This hypothesis implies that a sequence of tasks can be written down in the same order as the logical operations and that children will successfully complete these tasks *in that sequence* as they grow older. Furthermore, tasks cannot be performed *except in this sequence* because of the psychological hierarchy, which underlies task performance and parallels the logical hierarchy of the operations. Table 2 summarizes this argument.

This sequencing hypothesis can be described as follows: The psychological state of the child is represented in terms of the presence or absence of the capacity to carry out each logical operation. Thus, the developmental state of the child can be arranged in the same sequence as the logical sequence of the operations. There are now three sequences that can be directly related to each other. In this schedule, shown in Table 2, zero means absence or task failure, and one means presence or task success. The triangle of ones is a direct result of the hierarchic structure of the operations and its mapping into the task structure.

Age and Psychological States: Stage Hypothesis. The psy-

67

The Development of Adaptive Intelligence

Table 2.

THE MODEL UNDERLYING THE SEQUENCING HYPOTHESIS

Psychological State	Logical Operation					Task Performance				
	I	II	III	IV	V	I	II	III	IV	V
1	0	0	0	0	0	0	0	0	0	0
2	1	0	0	0	0	1	0	0	0	0
3	1	1	0	0	0	1	1	0	0	0
4	1	1	1	0	0	1	1	1	0	0
5	1	1	1	1	0	1	1	1	1	0
6	1	1	1	1	1	1	1	1	1	1

chological states described above are related to the chronological age of a child because of the developmental hypothesis. That is, the states are entered by children in the same sequence as they are numbered. This implies that there is a relationship—between the probability of being in a given psychological state and chronological age—which is monotonically increasing. This is assured by the constraint imposed on development, which prohibits backward movement, that is, regression, through states.

The nature of these psychological states is such that they are entered "all at once." This implies that the age relation includes, for a given homogeneous population, a small age interval in which the probability of being in a given state rises very rapidly. Figure 4 depicts this age by state probability relationship most directly. In the example illustrated by Figure 4, the age interval from four to five years includes the jump in the probability of being in state X. This jump reflects the hypothesis that such states are entered all at once by a child, rather than gradually, and that homogeneous populations have similar developmental schedules.

The sequence of psychological stages that is hypothesized

The Results

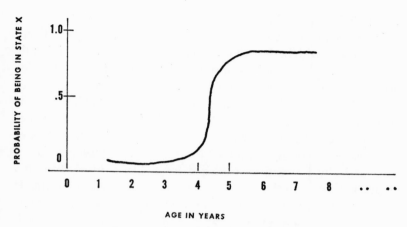

FIGURE 4. Staging hypothesis.

has a further implication in terms of chronological age. The midpoints of these jumps in age intervals can be ordered in the same way as psychological states. Finally, because the psychological stages are defined as the capacity to perform a particular operation, the relationship between the probability of performing an operation and chronological age has the same properties as just described for states.

It should be noted that there are at least two possible criteria for the onset of a stage. First, one can look for the presence of significant differences in percentage of correct responses between two successive age groups (t-test). Before the onset of a stage, there should be random fluctuations around chance performance. At the age of onset, there should be a significant increase in correct responses, followed thereafter by random fluctuations. A second criterion is a sudden shift from a minority to a majority of correct responses. If one can expect a high level of performance on the tests used to tap a given stage, then this criterion is a logical consequence of Piaget's assertion that all of the people in a homogeneous, well-adapted culture will evidence each stage at roughly the same time.

For the present data, these two criteria usually coincided,

so no choice had to be made between them. In general, however, it is necessary to consider carefully which criterion to use. There are problems with both of the criteria mentioned here, and it is only because their demarcations of stage coincided and therefore reinforced each other that we considered them adequate.

The first criterion suffers from the fact that many tests given to a wide age range will show significant differences between groups. Piaget's theory predicts such differences in homogeneous populations, but the presence of such differences cannot automatically be used as evidence for a hierarchical structure. Thus, the first criterion by itself is necessary but not sufficient. It must at least be supplemented by a logical analysis of the tasks at issue yielding a meaningful interpretation of any staging found.

The second criterion would seem at first to be a sufficient one. But, as already mentioned, it rests on the crucial assumption that one should expect a high level of performance on the tasks used to tap a given stage. For the lower stages of development, such an assumption is theoretically and empirically valid. Evidence for the universal presence of the later stages of development is not unambiguous, however. At the level of formal operations, the picture is far from clear. There is increasing evidence that the percentage of a population evidencing formal thought on a given measure is far from a majority in Western groups (Kohlberg and Gilligan, 1971; Jackson, 1965; Lovell, 1961). Furthermore, there is increasing speculation that some people, and even some cultures, never acquire formal abilities. In response to the evidence and speculation, Piaget (1972) has suggested that, although it is conceivable that the formal operations may not be universal, he prefers to consider them content-specific. Thus, a given person is only necessarily formal in his own area of specialization (such as navigation, tool-making, or physics) and may not have had sufficient interaction with the environment to have achieved a formal level in other areas. Such a situation would make the measurement of formal thought extremely difficult. Any given general test might be relevant to the skills of only a minority of a population and thus might show a low percentage of attainment of formal abilities. To use the criterion of passage from a minority to a majority of correct responses would then be a theoretically unjustified approach. It is clear that more thought must be given to these issues. In the present research, the problem of measuring formal abilities was not encountered, because the formal test that measured low-level formal abilities was passed by the majority of the older children.

In the analysis that follows, the two criteria discussed above were used jointly. Thus, passage to a new stage was defined as a significant increase in percentage of correct responses from a minority to a majority of correct responses.

Selecting Items for Analysis

Before presenting the experimental evidence supporting the stage and sequence hypothesis, it is necessary to discuss the selection of items in the analysis of data. Within the sections, the following questions are theoretically equivalent: Section I, questions i–m; Section II, questions n–p; Section III, questions a–d; Section IV, questions s, v, y, and cc; and Section V, questions k–m. Other items were not included in the analysis, because they were included in the test to introduce new concepts rather than to measure abilities. For the items listed above, the percentages of subjects at all ages who answered correctly are given in Table 3.

Although the items within each section are theoretically equivalent, all items within each section are not in fact found to be equally difficult. The discrepant items are the first item in Sections II, III, and IV.

In Section II, a distinctly smaller percentage responded correctly to item n than to the other two items. This depressed score on item n may result from the absence of an introductory question in Section II. Although the tasks in Section I may be solved by matching blocks horizontally, Section II, which appears with no break in format, requires that the subject analyze differ-

The Development of Adaptive Intelligence

Table 3.

CORRECT RESPONSES BY ITEM

Section	Item	Percent Correct
I	i	92
	j	94
	k	91
	l	92
	m	94
II	n	45
	o	64
	p	72
III	a	94
	b	61
	c	57
	d	64
IV	s	88
	y	56
	v	45
	cc	44
V	k	10
	l	13
	m	33

ences by mentally coordinating two sets of relations. Item n of Section II is the first such question, after five consecutive questions for which the correct answer can be supplied by matching.

Apparently there are some subjects who possess the ability necessary for Section II, but do not fully perceive the exact nature of its complexity until they are presented with the second item in the section. Although subjects who do not have the ability required in Section II would continue to match throughout the

The Results

section, the subjects who have the requisite ability but are caught unaware would respond by attending to only one of the two relationships on the first question of Section II. It was thought that these subjects would fully perceive the nature of the complexity of Section II by the second item. An analysis of the incorrect responses subjects give on the questions of Section II bears out this hypothesis. The percentage of incorrect responses that are the result of attending to only one of the two relationships involved in the solution decreases sharply from item n to items o and p. The percentage is 34 percent for item n, 19 percent for item o, and 15 percent for item p. These figures suggest that the low percentage of correct responses on item n of Section II can be attributed to the fact that some subjects who possess the ability tested in Section II are caught unaware by item n, and do not respond by coordinating two sets of relations between blocks until item o.

The other two discrepancies involve the first item in Section III and the first item in Section IV. Sections III and IV contain questions in which an operator cube is present, and the first item in both sections contains an identity operator. Although theoretically all of the operations are of equal difficulty, in fact, test questions involving identity are more often correctly solved.

Evidently it is far easier to identify the operation performed on two sets of relations when the two matrices involved each contain pairs of identical blocks (Section IIIa); it is also easier to operate on a relation when both the matrix produced and the matrix operated on contain two pairs of identical blocks (Section IVs). This may be attributed to the fact that perceiving two matrices to be identical does not necessarily involve the ability to infer a rule; whereas, with the other operators, it is necessary to apprehend a *difference* between the matrices, and so the rule that characterizes this difference must be inferred.

In Section IV, subjects who are unable to infer a rule may simply produce a relation, with the answer blocks, which is identical to the relation in the stimulus matrix. This simple non-rule-generated response just happens to yield the right answer to questions involving the identity operator, because the stimulus

73

matrix always consists of pairs of identical blocks. The only question for which this process results in a correct response is the one that involves the identity operation. It appears, then, that the identity operation question can be answered correctly by using a lower level ability.

This situation could account for the relatively higher percentage of correct responses on the identity question. An analysis of the specific incorrect responses given on these three questions bears out this hypothesis. In fact, by far the most frequent type of incorrect response to items v, y, and cc was an identity response. Of the incorrect responses, the actual percentage of identity responses given to item v was 52 percent; for item y, the figure was 47 percent; for item cc, the figure was 42 percent. Because a subject who performs the production tasks of Section IV by this method produces a relation that is correct only for the identity operation, the higher percentage of correct responses for identity can be explained by this tendency to reproduce the stimulus relation.

Pseudo-Items

Development. In order to evaluate the nature of the relationships among levels, some form of cross-tabulation of the dichotomous responses to items is required. However, because we have more than one item per level and only sixty-seven subjects, we cannot make a cross-tabulation of all items for all levels without having more empty cells than full ones. That is, with sixty-seven subjects there are no more than sixty-seven possible patterns of response over items observable, but if we cross-classified all items for all levels, we would generate 2^{10} patterns—clearly many more than could occur. There is no literature known to us that provides a method of analysis in such cases. We have therefore devised a procedure, which we have named the *Pseudo-Item procedure*, that at least allows us to answer some of our questions about the data.

In defining our Pseudo-Item procedure, we did not want

merely to randomly select one item from each level and use the single resulting string for all of our inferences. Clearly, by chance we might then pick the worst or the best performing string and thereby badly misrepresent the data in our inferences. On the other hand, we did not want to construct all of the thirty-two possible five-item strings and engage in complex calculation and model building in our main analysis. It should be noted however, that these complex calculations were carried out as a verification of the Pseudo-Item analysis, and the results are presented in the Appendix. The next subsection discusses our compromise.

Formation. Apart from the three empirically discrepant items discussed earlier, the items in each of the five sections of the test have similar percentages of correct responses and are theoretically equivalent. Omitting the discrepant items, two items were arbitrarily chosen from each section to use in creating the Pseudo-Items: items i and j from Section I; items o and p from Section II; items c and d from Section III; items v and y from Section IV; and items k and l from Section V.

The responses of each subject to each of the two items selected from each of the five sections of the test were treated as if they were the responses of *two* subjects to a *single* item; thus Pseudo-Items were formed. The procedure just described has the effect of increasing the N for each section of the test from 67 to 134, and thereby adds stability to the pattern of results (see the Appendix). The percentage of the 67 subjects who answered correctly or incorrectly on both of the two items in each Pseudo-Item is: P-I 1: 98 percent; P-I 2: 78 percent; P-I 3: 85 percent; P-I 4: 64 percent; P-I 5: 97 percent. The analysis that follows is based on Pseudo-Items.

Sequence and Stage Results on Blocks Test

Sequencing. The first hypothesis subjected to analysis predicts that the appearance of cognitive abilities follows a logically invariant sequence. Sixty-three percent of the subjects fall into one of the six predicted patterns. There are thirty-two possible patterns of response. The probability that the response patterns of 63 percent of the subjects tested would be limited to the six predicted patterns is 3×10^{-15}.

Staging. The second part of the Piagetian hypothesis predicts that cognitive abilities will appear in stages; there should be a reversal in the percentages of subjects performing correctly, from most subjects performing incorrectly to most subjects performing correctly at the age of stage acquisition, which is reflected in a significant increase at that and only that point.

The percentage of correct responses for the five sections by age are given in Table 4. The percentages in Table 4 bear out the stage hypothesis. All age groups possess the ability required to perform correctly on the questions of Section I; none of the differences is significant. The ability to perform correctly on Sections II and III appears at age ten; the only significant difference between age groups in performance on Sections II and III is found between the eight-to-nine and the ten year olds, distinguishing ten years as the age of acquisition ($t = 3.04$, $p < .01$, and $t = 6.63$, $p < .001$). The ability to perform correctly on Section IV appears at age eleven; only the difference between the ten and the eleven-to-twelve year olds is significant, thereby distinguishing eleven to twelve years as the age of acquisition for the abilities tested ($t = 2.29$, $p < .05$). None of the age groups performed correctly on Section V above the average predicted by chance—that is, above 25 percent, and none of the differences is significant.

The abilities necessary to perform correctly on Sections II and III appear at the same age (ten years). Sections II and III appear to measure two distinct facets of the same operational ability, because the percentage of subjects who master Section I but fail on all subsequent tasks except Section II (XXOOO, 9 percent) is approximately equal to the percentage of subjects who master Section I but fail on all subsequent tasks except Section III (XOXOO, 6 percent). There appear, therefore, to be two distinct sequences.

The sequence of abilities measured by the test items can

The Results

Table 4.

PERCENTAGE OF CORRECT RESPONSES

Section	Age Group[a]				
	8–9	10	11–12	13–15	16–19
	(N = 28)	(N = 26)	(N = 28)	(N = 30)	(N = 22)
I	78.6	92.3	96.4	100.0	100.0
II	32.1	73.1	71.4	90.0	72.7
III	7.1	73.1	75.0	73.3	81.8
IV	35.7	30.8	60.7	70.0	54.5
V	7.1	11.5	25.0	13.3	18.2

[a] The ages in the groups are assigned by rounding up from the half year. The means that follow are based on the resulting assignment to a whole year category. Mean age and range for each group are: 8–9, 8.5, 7.0–9.4; 10, 10.0, 9.5–10.5; 11–12, 12.25, 10.6–12.5; 13–15, 13.6, 12.6–15.5; 16–19, 17.36, 15.6–19.5. The distribution was created by testing virtually all children in Point Hope. Within each group subjects are equally divided by sex.

be considered to emerge as follows: The first stage is measured by Section I; the second stage is measured by Sections II and III; the third stage is measured by Section IV (and the Mixed Inputs section). Ability to perform correctly the tasks of Section V was not demonstrated by the Eskimo subjects. Figure 5 summarizes this sequence.

Treating Sections II and III as tasks at the same level creates two theoretically possible sequences. The first of these new sequences consists of Sections I, II, IV, and V; the second consists of Sections I, III, IV, and V. This revision adds credibility to the sequencing hypothesis. The percentage of subjects who support the sequencing hypothesis with Section II eliminated from the sequence is 74.65; with Section III eliminated from the sequence it is 76.8.

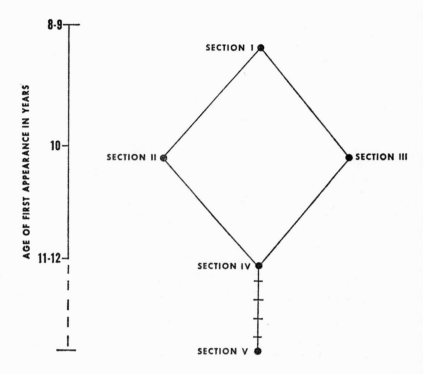

FIGURE 5.
Developmental sequence obtained on Sections I to V.

Mixed Inputs

The Mixed Inputs section consists of two subsections that are structurally identical to the subsections of Section IV of the Colored Blocks Test. One subsection involves the red (identity) operator and the other involves the yellow (shape) operator. The blue and green operations were omitted from the Mixed Inputs question to reduce testing time. The percentages of subjects who performed correctly on the Mixed Inputs items that correspond to the red and yellow items of Section IV are 71.7 (red) and

The Results

38.8 (yellow). The higher percentage of correct responses on the item involving the identity operator can be accounted for by the previously discerned peculiarities of questions involving the identity operator.

The percentage of correct responses on the Mixed Inputs question involving the yellow operation (38.8) is very close to the percentage of correct responses to the yellow item of Section IV (45). To determine the position of the Mixed Inputs questions within the developmental sequence, subjects' responses to the yellow items of Section IV and Mixed Inputs and a representative item of Section V were analyzed. Seventy percent of the subjects performed correctly or incorrectly on both the Section IV and Mixed Inputs items. Thus, it is highly probable that a subject who produces a correct response on one of the items will produce a correct response on the other. It appears that Section IV and the Mixed Inputs do not test different developmental stages although, from these data, the possibility that they may involve different abilities within the same stage cannot be ruled out.

To verify this position of Mixed Inputs in the sequence, it is now compared with Section V. Fifty-nine percent of the subjects performed correctly or incorrectly on both Mixed Inputs and Section V items. Of the subjects who responded incorrectly on one of the two items, 81 percent answered the Section V item incorrectly $(N = 22)$, and 19 percent answered Mixed Inputs incorrectly $(N = 5)$. Fifty-six percent of the subjects performed correctly or incorrectly on both the Section IV item and the Section V item. Of the subjects who performed incorrectly on one of the two items, 86 percent responded to the Section V item incorrectly $(N = 25)$, and 14 percent $(N = 4)$ responded to the Section IV item incorrectly. The above results demonstrate that Section IV and Mixed Inputs stand in the same relation to the Section V task, and that Section V was more difficult than either Section IV or Mixed Inputs.

The Development of Adaptive Intelligence

Analogue Results

Sequencing. The cultural analogue was constructed to parallel Sections I, II, and IV of the Colored Blocks Test, in order to measure the same cognitive operations with culturally relevant stimulus materials. In analyzing the analogue data, Pseudo-Items were created using the analogue items that corresponded to the items used in creating Pseudo-Items for Sections I, II, and IV of the Colored Blocks Test.

The hypothesis that development conforms to an invariant sequence predicts that subjects' performance on the three analogue sections will fall into one of four predicted patterns: pattern a, OOO; pattern b, XOO; pattern c, XXO; and pattern d, XXX. X indicates correct response, and O indicates incorrect response.

Ninety-two percent of the subjects fall into one of the four predicted patterns. The probability of four of the eight possible patterns occurring in 92 percent of the cases by chance is 10^{-13}. When Sections I, II, and IV of the blocks test are viewed in the same way, as though the results on these sections were independent of Sections III and V, 84 percent of the subjects fall into one of the four predicted patterns ($p = 10^{-8}$). Thus, the results on the analogue items support the sequencing hypothesis more strongly than do the corresponding results on the Colored Blocks Test.

Staging. The hypothesis that basic cognitive abilities will appear as stages predicts that the probability of correct task performance will increase sharply at the age of stage acquisition and remain fairly constant for subsequent ages. The age of onset of the abilities should conform to the developmental order of the tasks. The percentages of correct responses for the three sections by age are shown in Table 5.

The percentages in Table 5 demonstrate stage effects. All age groups are shown to possess the ability required for the analogue to Section I. The ability to perform correctly on the ana-

The Results

Table 5.

PERCENTAGE OF CORRECT RESPONSES FOR THE THREE ANALOGUE SECTIONS

Section	Age Group				
	8–9 (N = 28)	10 (N = 26)	11–12 (N = 28)	13–15 (N = 30)	16–19 (N = 22)
I	100.0	100.0	100.0	100.0	100.0
II	46.4	80.8	85.7	96.7	95.5
IV	42.9	38.5	60.7	86.7	68.2

logue to Section II appears at age ten; the only significant difference between age groups in performance on Section II is found between ages eight-to-nine and ten, distinguishing ten years as the age of acquisition for Section II ($t = 2.82$, $p < .01$). The ability to perform correctly on the analogue to Section IV appears at age eleven; the difference between ten and eleven-to-twelve year olds is significant, indicating eleven-to-twelve years as the age of acquisition for the abilities tested in Section IV ($t = 1.672$, $p < .05$). There is an additional significant increase in the percentage of correct responses to the analogue to Section IV at the age level thirteen-to-fifteen, from 60.7 percent to 86.7 percent. However, there is a later decrease at the age level sixteen-to-nineteen. These unexpected, significant changes are probably attributable to normal variation, which is enhanced by the small number in each age group. They do not represent a reversal in subject responses—from a majority of subjects performing incorrectly to a majority performing correctly—as does the significant increase between the ten and the eleven-to-twelve year old age level. With this possible exception in mind, it may be concluded that the age when each of the analogue sections is acquired is the same as the age when the corresponding blocks test sections are acquired.

The Development of Adaptive Intelligence

Effect of Cultural Factors on Sequencing

Issues basic to the validation of the theory have been considered. It is now appropriate to investigate additional factors which, although they are not essential components of the Piagetian hypothesis, affect its empirical investigation. The majority of factors that fall into this category are termed *cultural*. The effects of cultural factors are much less important for the purpose of theory validation than for cross-cultural comparisons; nevertheless, they have implications for the hypotheses tested here.

Intrinsic to Piagetian theory is the assumption that all humans have the potential to develop the abilities to perform particular cognitive operations. Thus, in testing the hypothesis that the appearance of these abilities follows an invariant sequence, an attempt was made to keep the testing procedure as culturally neutral as possible, in order to enable subjects to perform close to their innate potential. The test stimuli used were familiar; the test relied heavily on nonverbal instructions; the verbal cues were of simple construction; there was an extensive training section; new test concepts were introduced slowly. Despite these precautions, we realized that there were limits on the extent to which an interaction between two cultures can be free from bias.

In attempting to investigate the effects of cultural factors on the Piagetian hypothesis, one such factor was isolated—the subjects' demonstrated ability to attend to two attributes, color and shape. In previous tests administered to North Slope Eskimos, the subjects demonstrated the ability to attend to both attributes. However, the responses to the sorting task indicated that the subjects tend to perform shape sorts more readily than color sorts. Seventy-nine percent of the subjects performed a shape sort; fifty-seven percent of the subjects performed a color sort.

The relation of the subjects' attentiveness to color and shape in performing the sorting task to their conformity to

82

The Results

one of the predicted response sequences was investigated. It was found that, of subjects who sorted for shape only, 63 percent conformed to a predicted sequencing pattern;* of subjects who sorted for color only, 56 percent conformed to a predicted sequencing pattern; and of subjects who sorted for both color and shape, 70 percent conformed to a predicted pattern. The number of subjects ($N = 8$) who sorted for color only is too small to allow meaningful comparisons with those who sorted for shape only. However, the probability that a subject will conform to a response pattern predicted by the sequencing hypothesis is greater if the subject attends to both color and shape.

The demonstrated failure of the subjects to attend to color as well as to shape in the sorting tasks, and its relation to the sequencing hypothesis, were further investigated by creating three special item sequences. Items from Sections I, III, and IV of the test were grouped as follows: (a) items for which responding correctly involves attending only to color changes; (b) items for which responding correctly involves attending only to shape changes; and (c) items which involve attending to both color and shape changes. Examples of items that could be the first item in each of the three sequences are (a) color change: Figure 1, k; (b) shape change: Figure 1, o; (c) color and shape change: Figure 1, p. For Sections III and IV, which involve operations, the yellow operation changes the shape relationship between two sets of relations, the green operation changes the color relationship, and the blue changes both color and shape relationships. Thus, the questions of these two sections fit neatly into the appropriate sequences. Sections II and V of the test do not contain items that correspond neatly to one of the three categories; a representative item from each of these two sections was inserted to complete all three special sequences. Thus, al-

* These sequencing percentages are based on a sequence of all five test sections, with Section II preceding Section III as in the original sequential order. It is realized that the fact that Sections II and III measure abilities that appear in the same age range serves to lower these percentages slightly.

though the special item sequences are not pure with respect to color, shape, or color and shape changes, the influence on the special sequences of the three items that could be distinctly categorized was strong enough to permit interesting comparisons.

Subjects' response patterns on these three sequences conform to a sequence predicted by the sequencing hypothesis as follows: For the color change sequence, 54 percent of the response patterns conform to a predicted sequence; for the shape change sequence, 72 percent of the response patterns conform to a predicted sequence; and for the color and shape change sequence, 63 percent of the response patterns conform to a predicted sequence.

It has been demonstrated that an item sequence that requires the subject to attend primarily to the shape attribute (72 percent) corroborates the sequencing hypothesis more strongly than an item sequence that requires the subject primarily to attend to color (54 percent). A sequence containing items that require the subject to attend to both attributes holds an intermediate position (63 percent).

The percentage of subjects who perform as predicted by the sequencing hypothesis on the special item sequences was related to subject performance on the sorting task. This comparison was undertaken to ascertain whether the lower percentage of subjects who performed in accordance with the sequencing hypothesis on the color change sequence was in fact due to a failure to attend to color, or was due to some other factor, such as the order of presentation of the test items. For subjects who demonstrated an ability to sort for shape but not for color, performance on the shape change sequence was compared to performance on the color change sequence. For the shape sequence, 70 percent of these subjects produced response patterns that were predicted by the sequencing hypothesis; whereas for the color sequence, only 43 percent of the subjects performed as predicted. There were too few subjects who sorted for color only to measure their performance on the color and shape sequence. However, the performance of the subjects who sorted for shape only on the color

The Results

and shape sequences reveals a strong relationship between the demonstrated ability to sort and the percentage of subjects who support the sequencing hypothesis.

It has been argued that the aspect of the hypothesis which predicts that subjects will perform according to one of several response patterns (OOOOO, XOOOO, XXOOO, et cetera) is affected by the subject's tendency to attend to the attributes of the test materials. The effect of the degree of saliency of the stimulus attributes on the percentage of subjects who produce a predicted sequence is again demonstrated by comparing the response patterns to the analogue with the corresponding test sections. The percentage of subjects who produce an allowable pattern for Colored Blocks Test sections I, II, and IV is 8 percent lower than for the corresponding analogue sequence. The higher analogue percentage may be attributed to the fact that the culturally relevant attributes of size and habitat of arctic animals are more salient than the color and shape of blocks.

In order to pass the test, each subject must first correctly identify the stimulus categories being tested (color and shape) and then apply the cognitive operations necessary to solve the various problems. If the stimuli are consistently salient across each stage of the test, failure to sequence could be attributed to the nonhierarchical nature of the subject's cognitive operations. However, nonsequencing could also be the result of inconsistent attention to the stimulus dimensions across the stages. This inattention could result from such factors as the subject's confusion over test instructions or his use of other dimensions such as block position to solve the problem. For example, a subject who passed Sections I and IV of the test and not Sections II and III (an example of nonsequencing) might have been attending to color and shape in Sections I and IV but not in II and III. His responses might not sequence because he did not attend to color and shape in Sections II and III, rather than because his cognitive operations were not hierarchically structured. Therefore it is through inconsistent attention that sequencing percentage might be lowered. If the dimensions of the test are not highly salient, then they might

The Development of Adaptive Intelligence

not be consistently attended to. The salience of those dimensions could easily be affected by the degree to which they are familiar categories. In this way, to the extent that familiarity with the properties of the test stimuli is limited by culture, sequencing percentage might be reduced.

Thus, cultural factors, such as the saliency of the stimulus attributes, have been shown to affect the extent to which the sequencing hypothesis is corroborated. Nonetheless, in the Colored Blocks Test, Eskimos attended to both color and shape consistently enough to produce a highly significant sequencing percentage.

Effect of Cultural Factors on Stage

Validation of the stage hypothesis is partly dependent on the percentage of subjects who correctly answer each test question. However, only particular aspects of the subjects' response pattern affect its validation. The defining structure is a reversal in subjects' responses from a minority to a majority of correct responses, or a saltatory increase as a function of age in percentage of subjects responding correctly on a given item, preceded and followed by a plateau. Variations in performance do not affect validation of the stage hypothesis, if they do not affect the basic predicted structure. In particular, if the test materials were very unfamiliar to the subjects, the plateau level might be sufficiently depressed so that it never demonstrates a significant difference from the chance level of responding occurring before the age of acquisition. More minor variations could affect validation of the hypothesis if they were of different magnitudes for different items, as might occur, for example, if different materials were used for testing different ability levels within the same test. However, the possibility of differential effects from cultural factors across items is greatly reduced here.

The *level* of performance achieved after the appearance of the ability is not a true measure of the operational ability of the population tested. Rather, it is a function of the success of

The Results

efforts to eliminate cultural effects that keep subjects from demonstrating their true potential. Thus, a comparison of the plateau levels reached in the performance of two populations cannot be taken to reveal differential ability, but rather must be the result of the extent to which the subjects in both groups are affected by noncognitive, culturally variable attributes of the task.

A comparison of the analogue item percentages achieved after stage acquisition with the corresponding Colored Blocks Test percentages demonstrates the effect of varying degrees of cultural familiarity of materials. After each ability appears, a larger percentage of subjects perform correctly on the three analogue sections than on the corresponding Colored Blocks Test sections. For the five age groups at the plateau level on Section I, the average number of correct responses on the analogue is 6.5 percent higher than on the Colored Blocks Test. For the four age groups at the plateau level on Section II, the average number of correct responses on the analogue is 12.9 percent higher than on the Colored Blocks Test. Finally, for the three age groups at plateau level on Section IV, the average number of correct responses on the analogue is 10.2 percent higher than on the Colored Blocks Test. Thus, the Eskimos achieve a higher final performance level when the stimulus materials are highly familiar.

Another aspect of the stage data that is not involved in validating the stage hypothesis and that may be affected by particular cultural attributes of the population tested is the specific age at which the abilities appear. For all individuals within a genetically and environmentally homogeneous group, the rate of maturation would be quite similar. However, different populations may differ in their rate of maturation. Thus, cross-cultural differences in the age of appearance of cognitive abilities is not impossible; in fact, it is to be expected. Environmental factors may retard the appearance of cognitive abilities in extremely poor developmental situations. Conversely, an extremely enriched environment may actually appear to enhance the developmental rate, by enabling the child to actualize all of his potential ability at any given age. However, although extreme environmental variation may produce differential maturation rates for different populations, the age of appearance of a cognitive ability is apparently not related to milder variations in such culture-related factors as the familiarity of reasonably familiar test materials. The ages of appearance for the items in the analogue were found to be the same as the ages of appearance found for corresponding items of the Colored Blocks Test, and only the absolute percentage of subjects performing correctly varies. Because the analogue and the Colored Blocks Test are supposed to measure the same abilities, and the subjects are the same, any other result would have thrown the assumptions of test construction into doubt.

Because the age of appearance of a tested ability is not affected by the degree of cultural familiarity of the test situation, it is an aspect of the Piagetian hypothesis about which cross-cultural comparisons can legitimately be made. Comparisons between subject groups drawn from two populations might be expected to show differences in age of onset, which might be attributed to an interaction of differences in maturational and environmental influences.

Kentucky Corroboration of Alaska Results

Background. In order to corroborate the evidence for the sequence and stage hypotheses obtained in the Eskimo data, and to verify the invariance of these structures, the Colored Blocks Test was administered to fifty-nine subjects from Knott County in the Cumberland Plateau of southeast Kentucky. Ethnographic studies covering this region have been written by Caudhill (1963) and Weller (1965). These authors focus on the effects of the decline of manual mining operations and the unemployment and social problems that followed. In addition (a) the children of the Cumberland Plateau learn skills relevant to squirrel hunting at a young age and continue to hunt at least through late adolescence, and (b) the rugged terrain, poor road system, and strong family clans have produced an insulated and inbred

The Results

people. The subjects in the Kentucky sample were all residents of Knott County and attended one of three regionally consolidated schools in Hindman, Decoy, and Vest.

Hindman consists of a city block that contains hardware, drug, food, and variety stores, as well as a city hall and two churches. In addition to service-trade establishments, there are two educational facilities—the county high school and the Hindman Settlement School. The former has eight hundred pupils and is a geographically consolidated tenth to twelfth grade high school. The latter is a community-operated boarding school that provides sleeping quarters, meals, and a liberal quantity of regional history and mountain culture for children living too deep in the mountains to be bussed to school.

Decoy is situated northeast of Hindman at the "head of the hollow." The population of this mountain town is eighty to one hundred people. The center of town consists of an elementary school and a community center. The elementary school is a two-room school house divided between grades one to three, and four to six. The community center is a large building that houses looms, kitchens, and an assembly hall. Many of the families in Decoy are in strip mining or coal-related professions, and a number of others rely on government assistance. The families typically consist of two parents and three or four children living in a one- or two-room frame house.

Vest is located southeast of Hindman and is a small village with a consolidated elementary-secondary school. The center of town consists of a store and a gas station. The school is very large, with a student population in excess of three hundred. These students are bussed in from the surrounding villages to attend the school. According to the principal and staff, many of the students used to attend school in smaller two-room school houses similar to the Decoy school, but recently the road system was improved, enabling creation of a consolidated school.

Staging and Sequencing. The most minimal demonstration of cognitive structure necessary for validation involves Sections I, II, and IV, because these three sections measure the first,

The Development of Adaptive Intelligence

second, and third developmental stages found in Eskimos. These test sections were used for analysis here as they were for the Eskimo test analogue.

The percentage of Kentuckians whose response pattern conformed to a pattern predicted by the sequencing hypothesis (OOO, XOO, XXO, XXX) was 96 ($p = 10^{-14}$). This is 12 percent higher than the corresponding percentage of Eskimo subjects and is a strong corroboration of the invariance of the sequence.

Table 6.

PERCENTAGE OF CORRECT RESPONSES IN THE KENTUCKY
SAMPLE FOR THE THREE COLORED BLOCKS SECTIONS

Section	Age Group[a]				
	8–9 (N = 24)	10 (N = 24)	11–12 (N = 24)	13–15 (N = 22)	16–19 (N = 24)
I	100.0	95.8	100.0	100.0	100.0
II	34.8	79.2	88.0	86.4	100.0
IV	43.5	41.7	68.0	54.5	75.0

[a] The ages are in whole years due to incomplete information on birthdates. Within each age group, the subjects are equally divided by sex. The distribution of Eskimo subjects was matched as closely as possible. The mean and range for each age group follows: 8–9, 8.75, 7.0–9.0; 10, 10.5, 10.0–11.0; 11–12, 12.33, 11.0–13.0; 13–15, 14.32, 13.0–15.0; 16–19, 17.0, 16.0–18.0. It should be observed that these ages are not rounded up from the half year as they were for the Eskimo sample.

The relationship of percentage of correct responses on Sections I, II, and IV to age for the Kentucky sample is shown in Table 6. These results bear out the stage hypothesis: for Section I, all age groups have the ability; for Section II, the ability appears at age ten ($t = 3.48$, $p < .01$); for Section IV, the ability appears at age eleven-to-twelve ($t = 1.90$, $p < .05$). There is some variation in the percentage of subjects who respond correctly

The Results

after the abilities necessary for Sections II and IV have appeared. In particular, the difference between the two oldest groups in Section II is significant. However, the 13 percent increase here is much smaller than the percentages corresponding to the other two significant differences, and seems to be an artifact of the test statistic, which is extremely sensitive to differences at the top of the range.

Thus, the Kentucky sample provides evidence for the invariance of the sequence and the staged nature of the abilities tapped by Sections I, II, and IV of the Colored Blocks Test. The percentage of subjects who produced a predicted response pattern was highly significant, and the percentage of subjects who responded correctly on a test section increases dramatically at the age of appearance of the ability measured.

Cultural Effects. The aspects of the results that are susceptible to cross-cultural variation can also be explored with the Kentucky data. The percentage of Kentucky subjects who produced a predicted response pattern is 12 percent higher than the corresponding Eskimo percentage. One possible explanation for this difference is the relatively greater salience of the stimulus materials for the Kentucky sample. A comparison of the sorting responses of the two populations supports this explanation: 75 percent of the Kentucky sample sorted for both color and shape, while only 45 percent of the Eskimo sample sorted for both. Because the salience of the stimulus attributes, as measured by the sort, has been shown to affect the percentage of Eskimo subjects who produced a predicted pattern, the larger percentage of Kentucky subjects who attend to both attributes during the sort may account for the higher percentage of Kentuckians who sequenced as predicted. This conclusion is consistent with the fact that children in southeastern Kentucky learn to attend to color and shape through an emphasis on both attributes in their toys, while Eskimo children do not have extensive experience with primary colors. Indeed, the recognition of form, the perception of distinct shapes against a background of ice and tundra, is far

91

more highly valued in the Eskimo culture and is more heavily emphasized in child-rearing.

The final aspect that could vary cross-culturally is the age of emergence of the tested abilities, which is a function of an interaction between maturational factors and any extreme environmental conditions, rather than of minor cultural variation. The ages of onset of the abilities measured were the same for the Eskimo and Kentucky populations. Thus, despite differences in the populations and their environments, the effect of the interaction between these variable factors on the cognitive development of the two groups is apparently the same.

Relating New Test to WISC Block Design

When a new test is developed, it is often compared with a standardized measure of similar abilities. This is necessary if the new test scores are to be used for making inferences about subject abilities, rather than simply to verify the theory from which the test derives. The comparison between tests is most valid on a sample drawn from the population on which the older test was normed. Hence, in the present study, the scores of the Kentucky subjects on the two tests are appropriate.

Because the comparison is only meaningful to the extent that the Kentucky subjects may be considered to have been drawn from the sample on which the WISC Block Design was normed, the Kentucky WISC Block Design scores were compared to the normative WISC Block Design score, by means of the procedure described in Chapter Three. When the individual raw score had been converted to its scaled score equivalent, means were computed for the age groups used in the study. The scaled score normative mean is always equal to ten. The Kentucky scaled scores were: nine-to-ten years, 13; ten years, 10; eleven-to-twelve years, 13; thirteen-to-fifteen and sixteen-to-nineteen years, 9. It is apparent that the Kentucky subjects are not too different from the sample of Scots on whom the test was normed.

The Results

The WISC Block Design scores used for the comparison are the raw scores computed from the WISC manual. For the purpose of comparing the new test with subject performance on the WISC Block Design, each subject was assigned a level—1, 2, or 3—as a function of whether he passed Section I, but not II and IV, or Sections I and II but not IV, or all three sections. The subjects who did not sequence could not be assigned a level. A subject's level was determined by examining his performance on one item from each section that was used. Because all items within a section are theoretically equivalent, one representative item was selected arbitrarily from each section: the first item in Section I, the second item in Section II, and the third item in Section IV.

The tests were compared by means of a one-way analysis of variance, where levels on the new test were the ways of classification, and WISC Block Design raw scores were the dependent variable. Subjects in the three levels were found to differ significantly ($F = 8.7$; df 2, 52; $p < .01$) in their Block Design raw scores. The differences between scores in levels 1, 2, and 3 were not linear. Level 2 subjects have the highest WISC Block Design mean ($\bar{x} = 31$), and the mean for the level 3 subjects approaches this value ($\bar{x} = 26$), while the mean of the level 1 subjects is distinctly lower ($\bar{x} = 17$). It may be concluded that, of the relationships explored here, the change from level 1 to level 2 functioning corresponds best to improved performance on the WISC Block Design. The two tests at most tap a partial common factor, because the change from level 2 to level 3 does not appear to have any counterpart in WISC Block Design performance.

6

Implications of the Research

The Colored Blocks Test was developed as a uniform set of nonverbal procedures and materials to test for the presence of the cognitive abilities thought to be central to each of three Piagetian stages. This test structure has the advantage that failures at any stage can be safely attributed to the difficulty of the stage, because it eliminates the possibility that unfamiliar materials or unnerving procedures will have differential effects at the different stages.

Moreover, the test is constructed in such a way that even preoperational children can answer all of the questions without guessing by using a preoperational rule. Thus, measures at all levels can be given to all children without frustrating or upsetting them. With data of this kind, we can judge how each child performed on the problems of each stage, independent of his performance on the others. Thus, children scored as preoperational were not those who simply failed tasks at higher stages, but rather were those who passed a preoperational task.

The use of nonverbal methods allowed us to use this test with two groups of children who would have been extremely uncomfortable in a situation where they had to explain their reasoning. More recently we have used a slightly modified version of the test with Hawaiian children who speak a "creolized" English. They, too, are notably reluctant to explain their thinking processes. Without a nonverbal test of this kind, we would have gotten very little data from any of these children, and we would certainly have obtained little unambiguous evidence for the advanced levels of operational thinking. Most important, having such a test enabled us to get away from testing for the presence of individual stages and to focus on the more interesting question of whether cognitive development is organized as an invariant sequence of stages, as Piaget has proposed.

In both the Alaska and Kentucky results, evidence is found in defense of the view that cognitive development is organized in an invariant sequence of stages. Results obtained more recently from 160 Hawaiian children of mixed ancestry conform quite closely to those presented for the other two groups.

Two issues concerning the results must be addressed. An obvious first question is whether the hypothesis of invariant sequence is adequately confirmed by a finding of 75 percent sequencing in an allowable pattern, as in the Eskimo results on the Colored Blocks Test. Given that there is considerable spread of sequences across the allowable patterns and that few children pass or fail all of the test, our answer is yes. It would appear that the 75 percent sequencing (see the fourth section of Chapter Five) accounts for enough of the variance so that we may safely infer that the main organizing principle is the predicted relationship among the stages.

On the other hand, the 25 percent of nonconforming patterns require some kind of explanation. The most likely explanation, in view of the data, is that cultural unfamiliarity with the materials and situations can and does account for these cases. We believe this because, when materials of greater cultural familiarity (the animal analogue) were used with the Eskimos, the allowable sequences were close to 100 percent. A similarly high percentage was obtained when the Colored Blocks Test was used with Kentuckians (for whom the materials were more familiar). In both of these cases, only Sections I, II, and IV of the test were given. The Eskimo blocks test sequencing percentage for these sections was 84 percent. This figure is distinctly lower than that for the Eskimo performance on the animal analogue (92 percent), or the performance of the Kentucky subjects (96 percent). The sequencing percentage for the same sections was 93 for the Hawaiians.

Unfamiliarity of materials could affect sequencing percentage through an inconsistent attentiveness to the stimuli as discussed in the section on the effect of cultural factors on sequencing in Chapter Five. This would tend to produce false negatives: subjects failing who could have passed. It is less likely to produce false positives. The probability associated with correct guessing is never greater than 25 percent in any test section, and in Section IV, for instance, it is far lower.

We do not think that many of the false negatives can be attributed to procedural problems. A flexible procedure was used, in which greater time and more trials were allowed if the child appeared puzzled. We are left, then, with an irreducible minimum of cultural difference that affects test performance.

The second question is whether one can claim to have demonstrated the presence of the two later stages (concrete and formal operations) since the data show achievement of those stages by distinctly less than 100 percent of even the oldest children. Again, we think the presence of the two later stages is demonstrated, and for similarly cultural reasons (as discussed in Chapter Five).

The stage-like nature of the abilities measured here is demonstrated by large and distinct jumps in the number of correct responses at a given age. Some children in any culture will fail because they were not paying attention or trying hard enough, or because they were frightened, or because they had to go home and were afraid to say so. Even in our own culture, the passing percentages are always less than 100 percent. The effects of these factors are obviously intensified in cross-cultural testing.

In addition, as Piaget has recently observed (1972), formal operational ability need not appear in all domains. The strangeness of the test situation for Eskimos increases the likelihood that test performance would be one of the domains where they did not use their maximum operational ability. Nonetheless, it remains possible that in fact fewer than 100 percent of these or other children actually attain the later stages. This would not bear against the stage-like nature claimed for the abilities tested. It might bear against a claim that the stages are universal, but no such claim is made here.

The research described in this book was conducted to gain evidence relevant to the hypothesis that cognitive development can be characterized in terms of an invariant sequence of stages in people who are undergoing successful adaptation, even if the form of adaptation in their culture is very different from the form in our own. This hypothesis, which we derived from Piaget, implies that cognitive development has a particular structure and, because of its interactive basis, that that structure will appear in (virtually) all people. If we had not found an invariant sequence of stage-like abilities, but Eskimos had successfully solved the problems in the test in some other pattern, or if we had demonstrated the predicted pattern in the Kentuckians but not in the Eskimos, we would not have provided confirmation for the hypothesis. We would, instead, have disconfirmed it. Confirming the hypothesis required finding invariant sequences of stages, and finding them everywhere. (It also implied that our prior assumption that Eskimos were successfully adapted people was correct.)

Remembering the adaptive mechanism from which the claim of universality derives, it is clear that some populations somewhere might not conform to the predicted pattern of growth. This would only be interpretable if there were other reasons to believe that such populations were not living in a state of successful adaptation.

Because our measures were new, our first inference from negative results would have been to suspect the validity of the measures. In particular, we might have questioned whether the sections of the test really did measure abilities characteristic of the Piagetian stages. This question arises in regard to Section V of the test. Even by our own criteria, Section V does not appear as a stage, despite our impression that the combinatorial task in Section V should measure the very essence of formal operations. According to Piaget, anyone who has acquired all of the formal operations should spontaneously realize the equivalences that exist among them as well as their group properties. Even though our operations are not the same as Piaget's, they are of the same level of abstraction (that is, they involve operations on propositions, and they have identical group properties), because our operations, like Piaget's form a four-group (Inhelder and Piaget, 1958).

Section V does not show, at any age, a distinct and significant increase to greater than 50 percent passing. This fact alone would not be disturbing, because no tests of advanced formal operations have found such large percentages of even late adolescents passing. More typically, the percentage hovers around thirty to fifty (see Kohlberg and Gilligan, 1971). However, in our data, less than 25 percent usually pass Section V, and that is below chance for our task. Moreover, there are no significant differences between adjacent age groups.

One obvious explanation for this finding is that there is something wrong with Section V as a measure of late formal operations, at least for these subjects. Somehow they are systematically misled to an incorrect formulation of the task. An examination of the data makes this seem unlikely, however. Although it is true that on the average only 25 percent of the children at any age solve Section V, our data indicate that, of those who get all of the items in Section IV correct (and who therefore presumably have all of the logical prerequisites for realizing the

Implications of the Research

group properties characteristic of the upper substage), 65 percent succeed on at least one of the items of Section V. The section does discriminate to some extent.

There are some problems with Section V, however. Most of the incorrect answers involve replacing a pair of operator cubes with a cube not in that pair. For example, the combination of identity and any other operator is that operator. The reluctance of the children to pick the same color cube as in the original pair may account for why they do worse on combinations including the identity cube than on combinations without it. In all other combinations, the correct cube is not in the stimulus pair. But successful performance on these latter combinations might be due to the increase in chance level to 50 percent when only two of the cubes are seen as possible answers.

Alternatively, given confidence in the validity of the test, the failure of Eskimos on Section V could be taken as evidence that the advanced formal abilities it measures are not universal and that Eskimos do not attain them. No such inference is warranted. Moreover, the defense for such an inference would have to be a denial of the universal value of formal operations in adaptation, an argument that we are not prepared to make.

One last possibility is that Section IV does not measure formal operational ability. In this case there would be no reason to think that Eskimos could perform at a formal operational level.

A complex concrete solution is possible in Section IV. This involves remembering a stimulus description of the output matrices used in the training task. Unfortunately there is no way to tell from their responses which strategy the children were using. However, we note that Section IV stages with the Mixed Inputs and later than the concrete problems in Sections II and III. These results strongly suggest that Section IV measures a stage distinctly later than concrete operations and is therefore at least a low-level formal operational task.

We can conclude with some confidence that Section IV does measure formal operations, but we are left with the finding that Section IV does not stage with Section V which, if it measures anything, certainly measures formal operational ability. Two interesting possible explanations for this discrepancy arise.

First, Section V may measure a much more advanced level of formal operations than Section IV. This account only makes sense if we have other reasons to believe that there might be substages in formal operations. Some evidence to this effect is offered by Kuhn, Langer, and Kohlberg (1971), who found such effects using a variety of formal tasks. Kohlberg and Gilligan (1971) discuss the possibility that there are three distinct substages of formal operations.

There probably are very distinct substages in formal operations.* Whether this implies that the later acquisitions are not universal or simply that they are not evident in all domains of functioning, as Piaget argues, is moot. Inhelder and Piaget (1958) make a distinction between two levels of formal operations, substages A and B. This distinction corresponds roughly to the difference between knowing some of the formal operations and knowing all of them, which implies noticing their group properties. In our test, each Section IV task involves the singular use of a formal operation, while passing Section V requires knowing all of them, because the group properties tested in Section V are only apparent if one knows all of the operations. There seems to be more to the story, however. Far fewer of our subjects solved all of the Section IV problems correctly than solved any one of them correctly (24 percent and 76 percent respectively). On the other hand, of the subjects who solved all four test items in Section IV correctly, 65 percent went on to pass Section V. It seems, therefore, that correctly solving all of the items in Section IV is highly predictive of solving Section V. If a subject does know all of the operations, he is likely to know the group properties. What is required to move from knowing all of them to seeing the group

---

* We consider that these abilities, as substages of the formal operational period, are not examples of horizontal décalage. The two substages do not differ in the generality of application of a fully acquired cognitive structure across various substantive areas, which is the most common use of "horizontal décalage."

properties is apparently some kind of representational ability, at least in our tasks. Whether or not formal operations B depend exclusively on operational abilities, as Piaget claims, it can be seen that Section V requires representational abilities as well as operational ones.

In order to handle the Section V task, the child might imagine and store representations of the effects of the first operator cube and then apply the second operation to that result as input. We know from the Mixed Inputs task that such inputs are not in themselves problematic for the child. Thus, the problem must be one of combining the operations in the absence of concrete representations of the effects of the cubes. The child's problem cannot be in a failure to remember the actions of each of the cubes, because he has the chart to refer to; rather, he is unable to create representations of intermediate steps toward solution. A child may be formal operational but fail on Section V if he does not have a parallel representational system suitable for encoding the results involved in combining formal operations. The children who passed Section IV and the Mixed Inputs questions might have been unable to do the combinatorial task of Section V, not because they lacked formal operational structures but because they lacked a parallel representational system for encoding the intermediate steps involved in computing the result. It can also be argued that a formal operational child would not apply the operations sequentially, but would reason on the basis of the actions of the cubes. In this case, too, an abstract representational system would be helpful, but for representing the operations themselves.

Thus, representation is apparently involved, at least in our task, in making use of the formal structures of substage B. A child may know all of the formal operations but need a representational system if he is to understand their group properties. In addition to its role in recognizing the group properties of formal operations, representation may be involved, in a more fundamental way, in moving from substage A to substage B. Perhaps under normal circumstances a child's active engagement in

101

representing the formal operational structures he encounters may facilitate his discovery of the entire set of formal operations or their full range of application. Thus, his representational abilities would aid him in realizing the full potential of his formal operational abilities.

The minimal role assigned to representational ability by Piagetian theory has been much disputed in recent years, especially by Bruner (in Bruner, Olver, Greenfield, and others, 1966). In Piagetian theory, representational systems are held to be no more nor, usually, less advanced than the general operational level of the child. Bruner has argued against Piaget's kind of interactionism, especially in assigning a more crucial role to the environment, and particularly to the linguistic environment. Bruner then argues that representation is somehow prior to cognitive development. The results obtained here suggest that normal representational ability may be necessary for some aspects of formal operations. Certainly we have no evidence that limitations in representational ability affect the emergence of formal operations. Such limitations may, however, be implicated in the emergence of substage B. The relevant representational skills may not always be automatically commensurate with the child's general operational level, particularly for dialect-speaking children.

A representational system appropriate to formal operational thinking might be provided by natural language or by formal representational systems such as the languages of science and mathematics. Clearly, few children learn a formal language unless someone deliberately teaches it to them. However, at least for bilingual children in a transitional culture, formal instruction may be necessary if even natural language is to be an effective representational system. This is because the child must develop a grammar and vocabulary sufficiently differentiated to permit accurate encoding of complex and specific, abstract ideas.

For children in a community where the parent generation, the expressers of complex ideas, usually speak a different language to them than the children speak among themselves, such differentiation may fail to evolve. Moreover, the child may

102

need specific instruction relating verbal expression to abstract ideas, in order to learn how to use language in the service of thought. Differentiation of language and ability to use language in the service of thought are not usually distinct in the real world. However, a child would need both of these abilities if he were to use natural language for solving problems like those in Section V of the test, and Eskimo children may lack both.

Eskimo children in the generation tested here are described by their parents as unskillful speakers of Inupiat. They are described by their teachers, as well as by standard measures, as unskillful speakers of English as well. Their English is fluent in the sense that they readily express ordinary events and desires. However, it is simple and undifferentiated, and Eskimo children have difficulty expressing complex ideas, or new ideas, or abstract ideas, with any degree of exactness. Structurally their language is a reduced version of standard English. In this respect it is not very different from the usual characterization of pidgin languages, although Eskimo English is not usually considered to be a pidgin or even a creole.

In addition, there is evidence for the view that the children do not readily use natural language in the service of abstract thought. Most of the children had difficulty answering probe questions administered after they had completed the Colored Blocks Test. Indeed, most refused to answer, and of the few who answered, none gave accounts sufficiently complex to have produced the correct responses they had just given. A child might account for a correct Mixed Inputs answer by saying, "See, red and blue."

The standard English in which the children are taught abstract ideas in school is very different from the English they speak among themselves. It is possible that their own language is not inadequate but merely too different from the language of instruction (Hall and Turner, 1974). They cannot think in standard English because it is not sufficiently comfortable, and they cannot think in their pidgin because they do not think of utilizing it for the kind of abstract reasoning at issue here.

103

The Development of Adaptive Intelligence

Research currently in progress has been designed to investigate these questions. We have given a battery of linguistic and cognitive tests to the children of a community in Hawaii where a creole derived from pidgin English is widely spoken. The linguistic tests consist of measures of competence (imitation tasks) in both pidgin and standard English, as well as production measures consisting of naturalistic speech samples. Two new sections were added to the Colored Blocks Test that are similar to Section IV, but which can only be solved correctly through formal reasoning. In addition to the Colored Blocks Test, the cognitive measures include two of Piaget's measures of formal operations. We have also added to the test a section that attempts to look at problems of storage and access. We hope to be able to determine the highest level of functioning of the children who sequence correctly. Through the use of tests that tap their ability to utilize structures at that level in new contexts, we hope to be able to determine whether speaking a creole affects the emergence of late formal operations or, alternately, whether it affects the ability to access formal operations.

Regardless of whether it is the emergence of formal operations or their accessing which depends on an available system of representation, children without such a system may be at a serious disadvantage. If children who do not speak the language of school instruction were taught to speak fluently, their ability to utilize advanced operational structures might increase.

In the absence of any hard evidence that formal operations are not universal, one can assume that they have some adaptive value. We know that they can be of adaptive value in modern America, where Alaskan Eskimos must now survive. Because of an assumed adaptive value, it may be desirable to consider how educational processes might facilitate the emergence of formal operations in these children. The goal is not to move them from concrete to formal operations, because most of these adolescents demonstrate the attainment of at least low-level formal operations. The problem is to facilitate the utilization of formal operational structures.

Implications of the Research

Eskimo children might be taught to differentiate their use of language further in school, and they might be shown relations between verbal expression and abstract ideas which would aid them in seeing how language may be used to encode abstract ideas. In fact, although there are highly specialized English courses in high school, no particular effort to teach expression which is both complex and accurate is made.

The curriculum in Eskimo schools seems much lower powered than is usual in high schools. There are virtually no hard core academic courses in which a child might acquire technical languages. Many children take no science at all, and many are distressed because they cannot take mathematics each year. It is clear that there is little opportunity for the children to acquire formal representational systems.

The teachers cannot be blamed for these problems, if indeed they are as widespread as we perceive them to be. Teachers are only trained to teach high school English, or history, or whatever, to children who speak high school English; the readings, the lectures, and even the ideas are so geared. Because the children do not speak English at this level, the teacher cannot function in the usual way. After several years of trying to invent a creative curriculum that would circumvent the problem, many teachers resign themselves to teaching vocabulary basic to their subject matters, rather than the subject matter itself. It is unfortunate that, because the children need a more intensive kind of instruction in English, the teachers fail to reach a point at which they feel comfortable in manipulating the concepts they have been at such great pains to introduce.

Thus, there is a vicious cycle. The children's English language deficit necessitates a minimally abstract curriculum, for which they need not extend their working use of English, and so the children do not learn to use ordinary language in the service of thought, and they do not acquire other, more formal, representational systems. A number of concrete suggestions for the planning of Eskimo education can be derived from the results of this study.

The Development of Adaptive Intelligence

First, Eskimo children are bright. If they need a special curriculum, it should be one that is geared to their particular language problem and presents extensive language training, to enable the presentation of abstract ideas. The children are bored in school, probably because they are not presented with enough material at a sufficiently high level of abstraction to keep their minds engaged. The problem of curriculum planning is often seen as one of providing for disadvantaged students. We suggest that the curriculum problem should be seen as the difficult task of providing a high quality academic education to students who enter school speaking an English which is, both grammatically and lexically, insufficiently differentiated to permit the use of standard instructional procedures.

Second, Eskimo children are unable to use the formal operational thinking that they have available in contexts that require a parallel language system. A curriculum for Eskimo children should address this particular problem. A major emphasis should be placed on teaching the children to learn to represent their abstract ideas linguistically. If the curriculum were more abstract, then children could be taught parallel language representations at every level.

Beginning as early as elementary school, an effort should be made to introduce simple, abstract ideas and to teach the child to associate those ideas with accurate verbal descriptions. He should be encouraged to do this without regard for whether the language he uses is standard English in its grammar and vocabulary, so that talking about his ideas is not inhibited by discomfort with standard English.

In high school, advanced vocabulary and grammar could be introduced to help the children express, in a more differentiated way, the new and more complex ideas they have at that age. This introduction might coincide with the child's felt need for having more that he wants to say, especially if he had already seen, through his education in elementary school, the facilitating effects of language on thought. When this special language supplement is introduced, it should be an intensive experience, presented during the first months of the first year in high school. This would increase the likelihood that eventually teachers would be able to teach solid academic classes in the usual way, and it would reduce the tendency for courses to become English vocabulary classes, as they are at present.

The test results, at best, have implications only for the structuring of the academic aspects of the curriculum. Indeed, the most problematic aspects of Eskimo high school education at present may not involve the curriculum at all. During a visit paid in the fall of 1970 to one of the boarding high schools, a great deal of home sickness and unhappiness with the living conditions was reported by the children. In spite of the good intentions of much of the staff, life for a child is not pleasant, and, as the children say, is "too different" from life at home. The barrack existence, coupled with the lack of privacy and high noise level, contrasts sharply with the close-knit Eskimo family life. At home, heavy emphasis is placed on independence and responsibility; at school, conformity to what appear to the child to be arbitrary rules reaches a level at which individual pride and initiative are stifled. Ordinary human activities such as sleeping until seven o'clock in the morning, making coffee, and being allowed out at night are considered privileges and are allowed only for good behavior. Although great changes have been made since 1970, it is still difficult to tell whether the children's poor showings in high school relative to their abilities should be attributed more to general unhappiness or to the curriculum.

Running through our data is occasionally a suggestion of a decrease in performance in the last age groups; this is particularly marked in performance on Section IV. The Kentucky subjects do not show this pattern, so it probably cannot be attributed to the nature of the task. These findings support the notion that the school experience, as it is presently organized, is, at best, minimally beneficial.

A new school for the North Slope, on the North Slope, is

being planned. It is hoped that the children will be less unhappy in this more familiar environment closer to home. It is only because there is reason to be optimistic about the far more serious problems of setting and context that an interest in curricular reform can be justified at this time.

Appendix

Statistics for Use in Measuring the Development of Qualitative Characteristics

This appendix is concerned with data. First, a problem is described that is relevant to qualitative measurement error and inference about a developmental hypothesis. An approach to this problem is then presented and used to analyze the items studied here, in order to develop a scale and evaluate its theoretical tenability.

There is a two-fold problem in verifying a structural theory of cognitive development through only systematic measurement—that is, in the absence of control over developmental events. The first aspect of the problem involves the uncertainty about the purity (*error-free* character) of each measure used to assess a particular cognitive capacity. Classical psychometric theory would consider the relative contribution of error variance

109

to total variance in this respect (expressed as the reliability, or more precisely, the generalizability of the measure). The second aspect of the problem involves a parallel uncertainty about the truth of the postulated theoretical relationships among the cognitive capacities. This two-sided uncertainty results in a fundamental and logically unresolvable state of ignorance when data is gathered using uncertain measures to verify theoretical relationships hypothetically underlying the relationships among the measures: Given disconfirming results, is the theory incorrect, or are the measures inadequate with respect to the capacities of interest? Only through a priori restrictions imposed on the analysis can this ambiguity be resolved, either by restrictions on the quantity of error in the observations (measures) or by restrictions on the theoretically admissible relationships among the measures. In the absence of such restrictions, however, it is still possible to deal statistically with the problem.

Any attempt to establish empirically an adequate set of measurement procedures for the basic cognitive capacities discussed by Piaget must cope with the above mentioned uncertainty. That is, (a) the reliability of the measures must be established, and (b) the validity of this hypothesized theoretical relationship among the various measures must be determined. This analysis dealt with problem (a) by taking each string of items permissible under the assumption that the cognitive sequence hypothesis is true, and by evaluating the variance in the percent admissible sequence patterns produced by substituting for any given item the other item in that Section. If a low variance results from such a substitution, this would indicate that the two items measure the same underlying construct. The analysis dealt with problem (b) by examining the average or typical interitem relationship over all possible item strings.

The preceding chapters have described in detail the nature of the measurement procedures. The tasks developed for assessing cognitive capacity can be divided into five sections based on their logical complexity. Within each of these sections, more than one item was used. If the measurement procedures are in fact equivalent, as they should be by theory within each section, then a strong relationship between the items within each section should exist. Furthermore, the observed incidence of theoretically admissible sequence patterns should not change as items within sections are changed. This is clear in the case of a perfect equivalence of item responses within each section, because, in such a case, there would be an exact parallel of response patterns over all five sections, no matter which item was used in a given section.

The question of measurement adequacy, or item purity, can therefore be evaluated in one of two ways. First, a simple cross-tabulation of the pair of items within each section can be made, as was done in Chapter Five. To the extent that a perfect correspondence does not exist for a particular pair, there is evidence that the items are not equivalent measures of the same underlying state. Such a cross-tabulation, however, does not provide information about which of the two items is a better measure of the cognitive capacity.

The second method for evaluating the quality of items as measures involves the systematic study of the complete set of response patterns for each possible string of items. Because either of the two items within a section can be used to generate a set of patterns, there are $2^5 = 32$ possible sets of patterns. That is, a pattern of five items can be constructed in thirty-two different ways, depending on which particular items are used together. Of these thirty-two patterns, only the six that are consistent with the theoretical hierarchy of cognitive capacities (see Chapter Five) are allowable under perfect measurement conditions. By computing, with the single sample of subjects, the proportion of cases exhibiting theoretically admissible response patterns for each of the thirty-two possible five item strings, comparisons can be made of items both within and between sections in terms of their effect on this percentage measure of scalability or theoretically correct cognitive behavior. This approach to item evaluation has an advantage over the previously mentioned cross-tabulation within sections. This second approach provides information about the

111

The Development of Adaptive Intelligence

improvement in the criterion used to evaluate theory due to an item within a section pair. Therefore, a judgment can be made about which item within a pair is a better measure of the cognitive capacity—which item improves the evidence (percent admissible patterns) supporting the theory. We have chosen, in this appendix, to focus on this second method as the most desirable practical approach to item evaluation.

The method chosen to evaluate item quality requires a number of steps. First, each of the thirty-two possible five item strings must be specified, and the corresponding percentage of admissible patterns actually obtained must be computed (n = 67). This result is given in Table 7. Here, each string is referred to by a cell number. The columns labeled Section I to Section V represent cognitive capacity levels, and the rows give the specific item in each section used to define that string (cell number).

For purposes of later analysis, there is an additional entry in this table, the log-odds for the cell. This number is the natural log of the ratio of the percent admissible to the percent inadmissible patterns observed for that cell. As can be seen from inspecting either the percent or log-odds column, there is variation in this criterion measure over item strings.

A summary of the percent entries in Table 7 is given in Figure 6. Each item is used to present the distribution effects of switching items within a section on the resulting percentages of admissible patterns. Items are judged incomparable in direct proportion to the tendency for the percent criterion to shift up or down with one of the items *no matter what items are used from other sections.* Thus, Sections I and V are equally well measured by each item, because there is nearly complete overlap of the criterion distributions. This figure also shows that there is a clear superiority of item y over item v in Section IV. The items in Section II appear to be nearly equivalent, but there are more item strings in which item o is superior to p than the reverse. Finally, in Section III, item c yields the highest percent admissible response patterns in seven strings; but because this is only in particular contexts, it is not accurate to unconditionally infer that item d is inferior.

Table 7.
Item Strings, Percents, and Log-odds

Cell Number	Section I	Section II	Section III	Section IV	Section V	Percents	Log-Odds
1	i	o	c	v	k	62.7	.519
2	i	o	c	v	l	61.2	.457
3	i	o	c	y	k	73.2	.993
4	i	o	c	y	l	71.7	.928
5	i	o	d	v	k	61.2	.457
6	i	o	d	v	l	44.8	−.222
7	i	o	d	y	k	68.7	.789
8	i	o	d	y	l	67.2	.718
9	i	p	c	v	k	61.2	.457
10	i	p	c	v	l	61.2	.457
11	i	p	c	y	k	71.7	.928
12	i	p	c	y	l	56.8	.278
13	i	p	d	v	k	61.2	.457
14	i	p	d	v	l	61.2	.457
15	i	p	d	y	k	62.7	.519
16	i	p	d	y	l	68.7	.789
17	j	o	c	v	k	62.7	.519
18	j	o	c	v	l	61.2	.457
19	j	o	c	y	k	73.2	1.008
20	j	o	c	y	l	71.7	.932
21	j	o	d	v	k	62.7	.519
22	j	o	d	v	l	61.2	.457
23	j	o	d	y	k	68.7	.789
24	j	o	d	y	l	67.2	.718
25	j	p	c	v	k	61.2	.457
26	j	p	c	v	l	61.2	.457
27	j	p	c	y	k	71.7	.928
28	j	p	c	y	l	71.7	.928
29	j	p	d	v	k	62.7	.519
30	j	p	d	v	l	62.7	.519
31	j	p	d	y	k	68.7	.789
32	j	p	d	y	l	68.7	.789

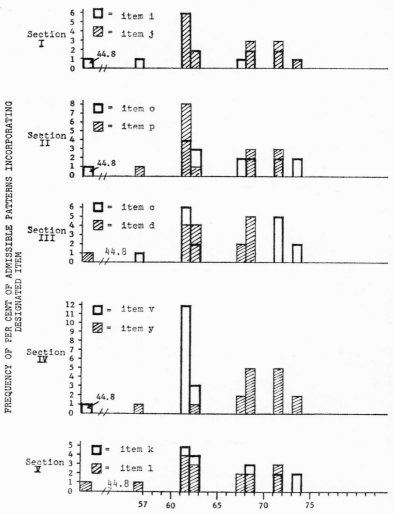

FIGURE 6.   Percent admissible pattern by section.

The manner in which the item strings have been defined—
that is, the systematic joining of each item with every other item
over sections—allows for the analysis of the variation in percent admissible patterns in terms of a factorial design. Goodman (1970)

114

and Theil (1970) present a rather nontechnical description of a method for analyzing percentage or count data under a linear model structure similar to those used in the analysis of factorial experiments. In the present analysis, the differences in the percentage criterion can be attributed to either item within section main effects (that is, the simple difference in the criterion percentage between the two items within a section), or to interactions among sections (that is, the unique increase or decrease in the percent criterion measure in strings with particular combinations of items).

The use of the log-odds transformation of the percent criterion for each string is very useful in a factorial design analysis, because the differences in the log-odds measures associated with the effect parameters computed under the linear model reflect ratios of percentage subtables (for example, the three way subtable of Section I by Section II by percent admissible response patterns). That is, differences in logs directly correspond to the log of a ratio—that is, $\log a/b = \log a - \log b$. Thus, the main effect for the Section I items in the log-odds measures directly reflects the ratio of the percent admissible patterns for strings with item i to that percentage criterion for strings with item j. There is an additional advantage of the log-odds transformation. When using percents, it is possible to obtain effect parameter estimates that imply values of the dependent variable outside of the $(0,1)$ interval. Such results are clearly inadmissible and are avoided by using log-odds.

The results of the analysis of factorial design effects are presented in Table 8. The effects are labeled as follows: Section I = A, Section II = B, Section III = C, Section IV = D, and Section V = E. Thus, the A effect is the difference in the criterion measure between strings including item i from Section I and those including item j. An effect with multiple letters as a label is an interaction. The AB effect is the difference of the A effect when item o is used versus item p from Section II. The table includes a column for the simple differences among percents as well as the log-odds measures. The entries in the columns do not correspond

115

The Development of Adaptive Intelligence

Table 8.

ESTIMATED EFFECT PARAMETERS FOR ITEMS

Effects	Percents	Log-Odds
A	−7.39	−.32
B	1.06	−.06
C	6.36	.29
D	−23.33	−1.04
E	6.24	.27
AB	1.06	.05
BC	6.8	.291
AD	0.6	.211
AE	4.6	.187
AC	3.2	.137
BD	−6.9	−.293
BE	3.5	.145
CD	−1.1	−.071
CE	1.1	.053
DE	1.1	.03
ABC	4.8	.171
ABD	−3.2	−.3
ABE	1.1	.039
ACD	1.06	.436
ACE	−6.33	−1.237
ADE	1.06	.490
BCD	1.06	.436
BCE	−5.8	−1.179
BDE	4.2	.170
CDE	−6.33	−1.237
ABCD	1.06	.500
ABCE	15.30	−.794
BCDE	1.1	−.108
CDEA	−6.4	−.269
ABDE	4.2	.177
ABCDE	1.1	.108

to differences in mean criterion, but the mean difference can be obtained by multiplying each entry by .35.

This analysis of the variation in percent admissible patterns in terms of items used to define strings can be used to decide whether any particular patterns of items are sufficiently better or worse than any others. The device chosen here to support such decision-making is the half-normal plot (Daniel, 1959). Normal probability paper is used, after some adjustments are made, to plot the effects in order of absolute magnitude. This technique is useful when there are no replicates to use in estimating an error variance, or when some evidence is needed to justify the use of high order interaction effects in error variance estimation. Figure 7 gives the half-normal plots for the effects using log-odds and percents.

This plotting procedure is useful for detecting very large effects and obtaining approximate error estimates. It is not a foolproof procedure, nor one which is always interpretable. It is used here because it provides simple visual evidence of specific effects under the log-odds analysis and shows the instability of the analysis using percents. A simple key to interpreting a plot involves fitting a straight line to the points. If all effects are simply the result of error—that is, if there are no non-zero effects—then the points will all fall on a straight line, the slope of which can be used to estimate the error variance. Departures from such a straight line at the top of the plot suggest real or non-zero effects, while departures at the bottom or middle of the plot suggest a serious problem of homogeneity in distributions.

The plot of effects based on percents indicates that there is not a simple error distribution which underlies this data and reflects the nonnormality of the error distribution for percents. Conversely, the log-odds plot conforms nearly to a straight line through point number 27. This gives evidence on an empirical level of the desirability of the log-odds transformation. Furthermore, the following effects appear significant: D, ACE, BCE, and CDE.

This analysis, therefore, suggests that there is sufficient

117

The Development of Adaptive Intelligence

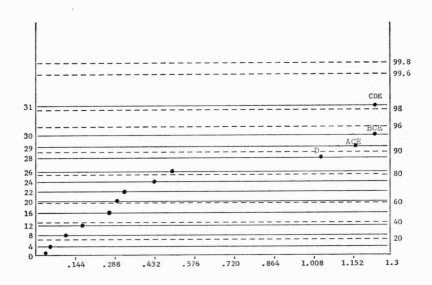

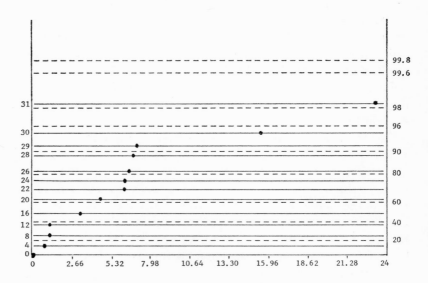

FIGURE 7. (a) Log-odds plot. (b) Percent plot.

118

evidence to conclude that item strings including item y from Section IV will yield higher criterion percents.

Furthermore, inspection of the three-way tables that underly the ACE, BCE and CDE effect calculations show clearly that strings using items [Section II, o; Section III, c; and Section V, k] or [Section IV, y; Section III, c; Section V, k] or [Section I, i; Section III, c; Section V, k] will yield the highest relative percent admissible patterns. Thus, there is evidence from this data analysis that relatively large gains in observed percent admissible patterns can result from use of specific items.

Finally, as discussed in previous chapters, the evidence relevant to the hierarchic structure of the item response process, and therefore, the underlying cognitive structure, can be found by evaluating the central tendency, over item strings, of the percent criterion measure—that is, the proportion of cases that exhibit the admissible response patterns under the sequencing hypothesis. Figure 6 clearly shows that the modal percent measure is 62. This number is resistant to the incidental or chance deviations in the percent criterion measure associated with items which we interpret as the measurement error characteristics of particular items.

Finally, the mean percent criterion is higher than 62 percent, which makes the inferences drawn on the basis of this 62 percent figure conservative. Furthermore, the 62 percent figure is based on an analysis that assumes that Sections II and III tap different levels. As discussed in Chapter Five, there is evidence that Sections II and III are merely slightly different measures of the same stage. The percent correct sequencing obtained with item strings containing either Section II or Section III, but not both, is 75 percent. This latter figure is probably a more accurate estimate of the percent correct sequencing.

Chapter Five presents a description of pseudo-items and results based on their use. It should be noted here that the pseudo-item procedure used in Chapter Five is simply one in which two of the distinct thirty-two strings of items analyzed in this appendix were randomly sampled and tabulated as though the two strings were separate samples ($n = 67$) of individuals responding to the same five items. This procedure has one, and only one, advantage. It is a simple and convenient way to analyze relationships among theoretical variables when the research design has more than one measure (item) for each theoretical variable (cognitive level) and all the measures are qualitative (dichotomous). The analysis presented in this appendix is the inconvenient but more precise way to resolve the multiple item qualitative measure problem in analysis.

References

BERRY, J. W. "Temne and Eskimo Perceptual Skills." *International Journal of Psychology*, 1966, *1*, 207–229.

BOCK, R. D., AND FELDMAN, C. F. "Cognitive Studies Among the Residents of Wainwright, Alaska." Paper presented at the convention of the American Association for the Advancement of Science, Boston, 1969.

BRUNER, J. S., OLVER, R. R., GREENFIELD, P. M., AND OTHERS (Eds.) *Studies in Cognitive Growth*. New York: Wiley, 1966.

CAUDHILL, H. M. *Night Comes to the Cumberlands: A Biography of a Depressed Area*. Boston: Little, Brown, 1963.

CHOMSKY, N. *Aspects of the Theory of Syntax*. Cambridge: MIT Press, 1965.

DANIEL, C. "Use of Half-Normal Plots in Interpreting Factorial Experiments." *Technometrics*, 1959, *1*, 311–341.

DASEN, P. "Cross-Cultural Piagetian Research: A Summary." *Journal of Cross-Cultural Psychology*, 1972, *3*, 23–41.

EELLS, W. C. "Educational Achievement of the Native Races in Alaska." *Journal of Applied Psychology*, 1933, *17*, 646–670.

FURTH, H. *Piaget and Knowledge*. Englewood Cliffs, N.J.: Prentice-Hall, 1969.

The Development of Adaptive Intelligence

GINSBURG, H., AND OPPER, S. *Piaget's Theory of Intellectual Development.* Englewood Cliffs, N.J.: Prentice-Hall, 1969.

GOODMAN, L. "Some Multiplicative Models for the Analysis of Cross Classified Data." In *Proceedings of the Sixth Berkeley Symposium on Mathematical Statistics and Probability.* Berkeley: University of California Press, 1970.

GREENFIELD, P. "On Culture and Conservation." In J. S. Bruner, R. R. Olver, P. M. Greenfield, and others (Eds.), *Studies in Cognitive Growth.* New York: Wiley, 1966.

HALL, V., AND KINGSLEY, R. "Conservation and Equilibration Theory." *Journal of Genetic Psychology,* 1968, *113,* 195–213.

HALL, V., AND TURNER, R. "The Validity of the Different Language Explanation for Poor Scholastic Performance by Black Students." *Review of Educational Research,* February 1974.

INHELDER, B., AND PIAGET, J. *The Growth of Logical Thinking from Childhood to Adolescence: An Essay on the Construction of Formal Operational Structures.* Trans. Anne Parson and S. Milgram. New York: Basic Books, 1958.

JACKSON, S. "The Growth of Logical Thinking in Normal and Subnormal Children." *British Journal of Educational Psychology,* 1965, *35,* 255–258.

KOHLBERG, L. AND GILLIGAN, C. "The Adolescent as a Philosopher: The Discovery of the Self in a Postconventional World." *Daedalus,* 1971, *100,* 1051–1086.

KUHN, D., LANGER, J., AND KOHLBERG, L. *The Development of Formal Operations in Logical and Moral Judgment.* Unpublished manuscript. Columbia University, New York, 1971.

LANTIS, M. (Ed.) *Eskimo Childhood and Interpersonal Relationships: Nunivak Biographies and Geneologies.* Seattle: University of Washington Press, 1960.

LOVELL, K. "A Follow-up Study of Inhelder and Piaget's *The Growth of Logical Thinking.*" *British Journal of Psychology,* 1961, *52,* 143–153.

MAC ARTHUR, R. A. "Some Differential Abilities of Northern Canadian Native Youth." *International Journal of Psychology,* 1968, *3,* 43–51.

MILAN, F. *Observations on the Contemporary Eskimo of Wainwright, Alaska.* Alaskan Air Command, Technical Report 57–14. Fairbanks: Arctic Aeromedical Laboratory, 1958.

References

MURRAY, J., WILEY, D., AND WOLFE, R. "New Statistical Techniques for Evaluating Longitudinal Models." *Human Development,* 1971, *14,* 142–148.

NASSEFAT, M. Etude quantitative sur l'evolution des opérations intellectuelles: Le passage des opérations concrètes aux opérations formelles. Unpublished doctoral dissertation, University of Geneva, 1963. (Also published by Delachaux and Niestlé, 1963).

PASQUAL-LEONE, J. "A Mathematical Model for the Transition Rule in Piaget's Developmental Stages." *Acta Psychologica,* 1970, *32,* 301–345.

PASQUAL-LEONE, J., AND SMITH, J. "The Encoding and Decoding of Symbols by Children: A New Experimental Paradigm and a Neo-Piagetian Model." *Journal of Experimental Child Psychology,* 1969, *8,* 328–355.

PIAGET, J. *Psychology of Intelligence.* Patterson, N.J.: Littlefield Adams, 1963.

PIAGET, J. *Genetic Epistemology.* New York: Columbia University Press, 1970a.

PIAGET, J. *Structuralism.* New York: Harper and Row, 1970b.

PIAGET, J. "Intellectual Evolution from Adolescence to Adulthood." *Human Development,* 1972, *15,* 1–12.

PRICE-WILLIAMS, D. R. "A Study Concerning Concepts of Conservation of Quantities Among Primitive Children." *Acta Psychologica,* 1961, *18,* 297–305.

RAINEY, F. G. "The Whale Hunters of Tigara." *Anthropological Papers of the American Museum of Natural History,* 1947, *41*(2), 231–283.

SIMON, H. *Sciences of the Artificial.* Cambridge: MIT Press, 1969.

SPENCER, R. F. *The North Alaskan Eskimo: A Study in Ecology and Society.* Smithsonian Institution, Bureau of American Ethnology, Bulletin 171. Washington: U. S. Government Printing Office, 1959.

THEIL, H. "On the Estimation of Relationships Involving Qualitative Variables." *American Journal of Sociology,* 1970, *76,* 103–154.

VAN STONE, J. W. *Point Hope, an Eskimo Village in Transition.* Seattle: University of Washington Press, 1962.

The Development of Adaptive Intelligence

VERNON, P. *Intelligence and Cultural Environment.* London: Methuen, 1969.

WELLER, J. *Yesterday's People: Life in Contemporary Appalachia.* Lexington: University of Kentucky Press, 1965.

WILKINSON, J., LUNZER, E., AND DOLAN, T. "Factors Affecting Cognitive Behavior of Children in Their First Year of Schooling." Paper presented at Biennial Meeting of International Society for Study of Behavioral Development. Ann Arbor, Mich., 1973.

Annotated Bibliography

This bibliography contains a selective list of landmark or representative studies relevant to the major concepts of the book.

Cross-Cultural Cognition

Major reviews and books of readings

BERRY, J. W., AND DASEN, P. R. (Eds.) *Culture and Cognition: Readings in Cross-Cultural Psychology.* New York: Barnes and Noble, 1974. This is the latest collection of readings in the area. It contains many crucial older articles as well as some previously unpublished material.

DASEN, PIERRE. "Cross-Cultural Piagetian Research: A Summary." *Journal of Cross-Cultural Psychology,* 1972, *3,* 23–39. This is the best summary available on the topic. Dasen has a good grasp of Piagetian theory and of the kind of evidence needed for a proper examination of its validity across cultures. He discusses evidence for the presence or absence of each stage, the horizontal décalages, and the substages in the acquisition of a given task. Finally, he discusses studies designed to examine the effects of schooling and European contact on Piagetian abilities. This article is a good source of information on unpublished work.

GLICK, J. "Cognitive Development in Cross-Cultural Perspective." To appear as Chapter Eleven in *Review of Child Development Research*, Vol. 4. Chicago: University of Chicago Press, 1974. This article is more important as a methodological framework than as the review article it is supposed to be. Aside from eloquent expositions of the current theories and research quandries, the article contains continued references to the view that cross-cultural cognitive development can be a fully justifiable discipline if the emphasis is placed on the study of "the performance determinants that govern the application of cognitive capacities, embedded in everyday life, to other situations."

LE VINE, R. "Cross-Cultural Study in Child Psychology." In P. Mussen (Ed.) *Carmichael's Manual of Child Psychology*, 1970, *1*. This is a good summary of work in all areas of psychology. The first section contains an excellent discussion of cross-cultural methodology.

LLOYD, B. B. *Perception and Cognition: A Cross-Cultural Perspective*. London: Penguin, 1972. This is a very good summary of the field. The research is discussed within conceptually well-defined categories that allow the author to draw conclusions about the current status of the major frameworks. The first two chapters contain a discussion of methodology.

PRICE-WILLIAMS, D. R. (Ed.) *Cross-Cultural Studies*. London: Penguin, 1969. A collection of some of the classics in the field.

Representative studies

COLE, M., GAY, J., GLICK, J., AND SHARP, D. *The Cultural Context of Learning and Thinking*. New York: Basic Books, 1971. This book is the first systematic attempt to examine closely the reasons for cross-cultural variations in cognitive skills. It contains a summary of on-going research and an eloquent presentation of a methodology that the authors call "experimental anthropology." The basic position is that cognitive skills exist universally, as evidenced by the skills needed in daily life, and it is the task of the researcher to explain why such skills do not appear in the experimental setting. This strategy is applied to classical paradigms of classification and problem solving.

GOODNOW, J. J. "Cultural Variations in Cognitive Skills." In J. Hellmuth (Ed.), *Cognitive Studies*, 1970, *1*, 242–257. Reprinted in D. R. Price-Williams, *Cross-Cultural Studies*. Harmondsworth, Middlesex, England: Penguin, 1969. The author attempts to synthesize the findings of a collection of cross-cultural studies, including those of Vernon, Greenfield, Lesser, Fifer and Clark, Price-Williams, and herself. She points to three major consistencies. She sees no overall lag, but rather a series of "peaks and troughs." Also, she sees the beginnings of consistencies in those tasks that are handled well or poorly by the various groups. In particular, she suggests that there may be problems with tasks requiring "imagined transformations."

GREENFIELD, P. "On Culture and Conservation." In J. S. Bruner, R. R. Olver, P. M. Greenfield, and others (Eds.), *Studies in Cognitive Growth*. New York: Wiley, 1966. This article contains an account of an elaborate study of conservation of quantity among the Wolofs of Senegal. The author varied the dimensions of cultural contact (rural-urban) and education (educated-uneducated). The results are discussed in terms of the type of justification given by the subjects. One interesting variation of the standard procedure consisted of asking the child to manipulate the materials himself. The resulting increase in conserving responses is discussed in terms of the attribution of magical powers to the experimenter.

LESSER, G., FIFER, G., AND CLARK, D. "Mental Abilities of Children from Different Social Groups and Cultural Groups." *Monograph of the Society for Research in Child Development*, 1965, *30* (102). This monograph contains the results of a large scale psychometric study conducted among children of high and low social class from several cultural groups in the New York City area. The general findings are interpreted to indicate that social class correlates with quantitative differences in skills, whereas racial group correlates with a difference in the patterning of high and low performance across skills. At

127

The Development of Adaptive Intelligence

present, the study is the subject of controversy, but it is still a good example of psychometric methodology.

VERNON, PHILIP E. *Intelligence and Cultural Environment.* London: Methuen, 1969. This is the best example of the psychometrician's approach to cross-cultural cognitive study. Vernon's aim was "to link up patterns of scores on different types of tests with differences of background." The test battery consisted of sections tapping verbal, inductive, Piagetian, spatial, perceptual, and creative abilities. The results of testing in Britain, Africa, Jamaica, and Canada are discussed in very general terms. The first half of the book is an extensive review of current theory and research.

Concrete Operations

Structure of concrete operational stage

WILKINSON, J. E., LUNZER, E., AND DOLAN, T. *Factors Affecting Cognitive Behavior of Children in their First Year of Schooling.* Unpublished manuscript. University of Glasgow, Scotland, 1973. The authors used a large battery of tests of language, learning, memory, creativity, and information processing, as well as standard tests like the Raven's Matrices and the Piagetian tasks of conservation of length and number, classification, class inclusion, and seriation. They report reliabilities and intercorrelations as well as multiple predictions of complex skills from simpler skills. They found that conservation loaded on its own factor, separate from the other measures of concrete operations. This finding is important in the light of the emphasis placed on conservation throughout the literature. For the classification/seriation test, the language measures were the best predictors. Significant social class differences are reported.

Classification and seriation

LOVELL, K., MITCHELL, B., AND EVERETT, I. R. "An Experimental Study of the Growth of Some Logical Structures." *British Journal of Psychology,* 1953 (62), 175–188. Nine tests of various aspects of classification and seriation were given to subjects aged five to fifteen, and the results supported the ordering difficulties postulated by Piaget.

SHANTZ, CAROL U. "A Developmental Study of Piaget's Theory of Logical Multiplication." *Merrill-Palmer Quarterly*, 1967, *13*, 121–137. Seventy-two subjects aged seven and one-half to eleven and one-half were given three tests, each of which was designed to tap a particular aspect of the groupings of concrete operations (classificational, spatial, or relational). Significant correlations between the tasks were found only for the seven and one-half and the nine and one-half year olds.

Conservation as a Phenomenon

FURLEY, LITA. "A Theoretical Analysis of Cross-Cultural Research in Cognitive Development: Piaget's Conservation Task." *Journal of Cross-Cultural Psychology*, 1971, *2*, 241–255. This article reviews the recent work done on conservation in other societies and proposes that performance on such tasks may be determined by two factors: (1) type of reasoning (empirical or magical), and (2) perceptual flexibility.

HALL, V., AND KINGSLEY, R. "Conservation and Equilibration Theory." *Journal of Genetic Psychology*, 1968, *113*, 195–213. In a methodological critique of conservation studies, the authors suggest that researchers are not always aware of the range of dimensions of variation across which a given conservation should or does apply. They report the results of three experiments using several conservation paradigms with new methods of changing the material in question. The results suggest that conservation is not as pervasive a structure as the typical experimenter assumes on the basis of the limited tests usually employed. Also, the authors' findings suggest that conservers (college students) are not as resistent to misleading nonconservation evidence as the equilibration model would suggest.

UZGIRIS, I. C. "Situational Generality of Conservation." *Child Development*, 1964, *35*, 831–841. A variety of substances were used to test 120 primary school children for conservation of substance, weight, and volume. The sequential attainment of conservation among subjects and across materials followed the order hypothesized by Piaget, although there were intraindividual differences (horizontal décalage) across materials.

Conservation as governed by Cultural Factors

DASEN, PIERRE. "The Development of Conservation in Aboriginal Children: A Replication Study." *International Journal of Psychology,* 1972, *7,* 75–85. This is a replication of the de-Lemos study, described below, using ninety children aged six to sixteen. The general findings were similar, with two exceptions. The quantity-weight reversal did not appear; nor did the difference in performance between pure- and part-Aborigines. Dasen argues for the environmental determination of the rate of attainment of conservation. He, too, found a large percentage of adults who showed no evidence of conservation.

DE LEMOS, M. M. "The Development of Conservation in Aboriginal Children." *International Journal of Psychology,* 1969, *4,* 255–269. The author tested all the standard conservations in two samples of Aboriginal children aged eight to fifteen (N = 145). She found a close correspondence between the answers and explanations of the Aboriginal children and those of Europeans, except that the Aborigines found weight conservation easier than quantity conservation. All conservations appeared later among the Aborigines. Furthermore, only 50 percent of the adults conserved quantity, and only 75 percent conserved length. The part-Aboriginal children in the same environment showed better conservation than pure Aborigines. This finding was discussed in terms of genetic differences.

MAHAR, J. S., AND JAIN, UDAI. "Development of Conservation in Rural and Urban School Children: An Experimental Study." *Indian Psychological Review,* 1969, *6,* 45–49. The authors found that conservation of quantity begins earlier among urban children. Contrary to Greenfield's findings, however, they found no difference between the two groups in the use of perceptual cues to justify judgments.

MERMELSTEIN, E., AND SHULMAN, L. "Lack of Formal Schooling and the Acquisition of Conservation." *Child Development,* 1967, *38,* 39–51. The conservation abilities (continuous and discontinuous quantities) of sixty American Negro children, six and nine years old, who had had no schooling, were compared to a similar group with normal education. There was no difference between the two groups on verbal and nonverbal tests of conservation. Performance on the nonverbal tests of continuous quantity was better than that on the verbal test of noncontinuous quantity. Because the order of difficulty is usually the reverse with comparable procedures for the two tasks, it was concluded that verbal questioning affects the percentage of conservers found.

PRICE-WILLIAMS, D. R. "A Study Concerning Concepts of Conservation of Quantities Among Primitive Children." *Acta Psychologica,* 1961, *18,* 297–305. This is still the most sensitive conservation study to date. The author tested conservation of continuous and discontinuous quantity among roughly forty-five children aged five to eight in the Tiv tribe of Central Nigeria. He used materials which were well known to the children (earth and nuts). The standard sequence of development was found, and there was little evidence for the usual age lag in acquisition.

PRICE-WILLIAMS, D. R., GORDON, W., AND RAMIREZ, M. "Skill and Conservation: A Study of Pottery-Making Children." *Developmental Psychology,* 1969, *1,* 769. This study is a dramatic example of the role of the environment in conservation. The authors tested twenty-eight children aged six to nine from two towns in Mexico. The children were broken down into two carefully matched samples according to whether they were raised in a pottery-making family. There was significantly more conservation of substance (clay) in the pottery group, but no difference on conservation of number, liquid, weight, or volume.

ZA'ROUR, GEORGE I. "The Conservation of Number and Liquid by Lebanese School Children in Beirut." *Journal of Cross-Cultural Psychology,* 1971, *12,* 165–172. Typical Piagetian conservation tasks were given to 224 Lebanese school children aged five to nine. The results confirmed that the ability to

The Development of Adaptive Intelligence

solve the problems increased with age, but the Lebanese age norms were found to be higher than those of Americans.

Formal Operations

Review articles

LOVELL, KENNETH. "Some Problems Associated with Formal Thought and Its Assessment." in D. R. Green, M. Ford, and G. Flamer (Eds.), *Measurement and Piaget*. New York: McGraw-Hill, 1971. This brief paper describes the nature of formal thought and reviews the extent to which research has corroborated Piaget's work in this area. Lovell points out difficulties in present research, particularly the role of content. The paper discusses the assessment of formal operations in the new British Intelligence Scales.

NEIMARK, E. "Intellectual Development During Adolescence." To appear as Chapter Ten of *Review of Child Development Research*, Volume 4. Chicago: University of Chicago Press, 1974. This is a very thorough review of the theoretical and empirical work done on the emergence of the period of formal operations. Although Neimark points out the lack of much definitive research on formal operations, she concludes that: (1) there is a stage of thinking beyond concrete operations; (2) this stage is not obtained by everyone and may not even be stable within an individual over time; (3) cross-cultural differences may exist in the attainment of these abilities; (4) within-culture variations also exist; (5) general intelligence seems to be an important factor in the development of these abilities; (6) individual variation in such areas as field dependence and memory may influence the rate of development and its final level of attainment; and (7) the effect of specific training procedures and techniques is an area for future research.

Replication studies

LOVELL, K. "A Follow-up Study of Inhelder and Piaget's *The Growth of Logical Thinking.*" *British Journal of Psychology*, 1961, *52*, 143–153. Two hundred subjects from primary school age through adulthood were tested with a battery of tests taken from *The Growth of Logical Thinking from Childhood to Adolescence*. The results generally confirmed Piaget's reports.

JACKSON, S. "The Growth of Logical Thinking in Normal and Subnormal Children." *British Journal of Educational Psychology* 1965, *35*, 255. Two subject groups, one of normal intelligence (ages five to fifteen) and the other of subnormal intelligence (ages seven to fifteen) were given problems taken from *The Growth of Logical Thinking from Childhood to Adolescence*. It was found that the ability to think at one level in a situation does not necessarily imply the ability to think at that level in other situations. Also, the low IQ groups showed little progress beyond age nine.

Structure of formal operational stage

BART, W. M. "The Factor Structure of Formal Operations." *British Journal of Educational Psychology,* 1971, *44,* 70–77. Ninety above average thirteen to fourteen year olds were given four Piaget formal tasks, four operational reasoning tasks, and one test of verbal intelligence. Two factors were isolated, one that was formal operational, and one that loaded on content factors.

KEASEY, CAROL T. "The Nature of Formal Operations in Preadolescence, Adolescence, and Middle Age." *Dissertation Abstracts International,* 1971, *31,* 7574. The author tested three groups of females—sixth graders, college women, and fifty-year-old women—on four Piagetian tests of formal operations. The subjects were pretested on the pendulum, balance, and flexibility problems. They were then given a training session and a set of post-tests consisting of the chemicals test, a revised flexibility problem, and a version of the training task. There was considerable stage mixture in all groups, but the sixth graders were predominantly concrete, the college women formal, the fifty-year-olds mixed. The incidence of high level formal operations was extremely rare. The training effects showed no generalization.

KUHN, D., LANGER, J., AND KOHLBERG, L. *The Development of*

The Development of Adaptive Intelligence

Formal Operations in Logical and Moral Judgment. New York: Columbia University, 1971. The section on formal operations consists of two experiments. In the first, 275 subjects aged ten to fifteen, sixteen to twenty, twenty-one to thirty, and forty-five to fifty were tested on the pendulum and correlations problems. The authors identified four major stages (preoperational, concrete operational and formal operations A and B) as well as substages within and between these four. The pendulum problem was reliably easier than the correlation. There is evidence that knowledge of the concept of correlation was not related to performance on the correlation task. After discarding twenty-five subjects who differed by four stages in performance on the tasks, the authors reported that most differed by only one stage. In the second experiment, seventy-five children aged ten to thirteen were tested on several formal tasks including pendulum, correlation, and chemicals. The pendulum problem was again easier than the correlation, and the chemical task fell reliably in between. There were twenty-six children at preoperations on correlation and formal operations on the pendulum. The authors emphasized two aspects of the findings. First, they argue for the presence of two distinct substages of formal operations. Second, they see evidence for a stable order of emergence of formal operations in the different contexts (horizontal decalage).

NEIMARK, E. D. "A Preliminary Search for Formal Operations Structures." *Journal of Genetic Psychology,* 1970, *116,* 223–232. Sixty-one fourth, fifth, and sixth graders were given three tasks. The first was a problem-solving task designed by the author, and the other two were Piagetian combinatorial and correlational tasks. Only the problem-solving task and the correlational task correlated with one another. An explanation was offered for this failure to find clear evidence of a structure of abilities.

Linguistic ability and formal operational ability

FURTH, H. G. "Linguistic Deficiency and Thinking: Research with Deaf Subjects, 1964–1969." *Psychological Bulletin,* 1971, *76,*

58–72. This article is a general review of the recent literature on deaf and normal children. The author concludes that the thinking processes of deaf and normal children are similar, at least up to the formal operational stage.

FURTH, H. G., AND YOUNISS, J. "Thinking in Deaf Adolescents: Language and Formal Operations." *Journal of Communication Disorders,* 1969, *2,* 195–202. Using a wide battery of Piaget-related tasks, five of seven bright but linguistically incompetent deaf boys aged thirteen to nineteen were found to possess some formal operational ability. This study concluded that linguistic knowledge was not necessary for the development of formal operations.

JONES, PAULINE. "Formal Operational Reasoning and the Use of Tentative Statements." *Cognitive Psychology,* 1972, *3,* 467–471. In this study, twenty-two pairs of boys aged eleven to thirteen, who were matched for IQ but differed in verbal ability and the use of tentative hypotheses, were given formal operational tasks. No difference between the two groups was found. This supports Piaget's view that level of cognitive development is not dependent on a concomitant level of language ability.

Stage and Sequence

Theoretical works

FLAVELL, J. H. "Stage-Related Properties of Cognitive Development." *Cognitive Psychology,* 1971, *2,* 421–453. Flavell discusses theoretical and empirical work done on four aspects of cognitive development: (1) stages involve qualitative changes in thought, (2) stages are characterized by abrupt development, (3) stages can be characterized as structures, and (4) the various items that define a given stage develop concurrently. He points out that quantitative improvements in such areas as memory, attention, and perception may be necessary conditions for certain cognitively qualitative changes, and that if a distinction is made between the commencement of a stage and its associated abilities and their

135

"functional maturity," various notions of gradualness versus abruptness, concurrence, and structure need to be reformulated.

KESSEN, W. "Stage and Structure in the Study of Children." *Society for Research in Child Development Monograph,* 1962, *27*(2). This article briefly reviews several uses of the concept of stage and points out that Piagetian, Freudian, and Hullian theories share the viewpoint that development consists of parametric variation of general formulations, although their basic formulations are different. A schematic representation of stage in terms of state, individual differences, and transitions is presented. The author argues that stage is a concept used to segment behavior into appropriate categories for further analysis according to what sort of behavior is to be observed.

PINARD, A. AND LAURENDEAU, M. "Stage in Piaget's Cognitive-Developmental Theory: Exegesis of a Concept." In D. Elkind and J. Flavell (Eds.), *Studies in Cognitive Development.* New York: Oxford University Press, 1969. This article presents the criteria used by the Genevan school for its particular concept of stage and development. The first criterion is that the stages are hierarchically arranged and follow an invariant sequence of development. The second criterion is that each stage presupposes, and is an integration of, the preceding one. The third criterion is that each stage is both a period of the achievement of new behavior and the preparation for the behavior of the next level. The fourth is that each stage is a structured whole. The fifth criterion is that each stage represents a particular form of equilibrative development.

TOULMIN, STEPHEN. "The Concept of Stages in Psychological Development." In T. Mischel (Ed.), *Cognitive Development and Epistemology.* New York: Academic Press, 1971. A noted philosopher discusses some basic issues in developmental theory. He concludes that (1) analytical epistemology cannot be adequately handled without reference to some aspects of the psychology of learning, (2) the psychology of learning cannot proceed without some well-defined analytic preconceptions, and (3) the notion of stage is at best a de-

Annotated Bibliography

scriptive convenience rather than a basis for discovering laws of development.

Empirical works

KOHLBERG, L. "Early Education: A Cognitive-Developmental View." *Child Development,* 1968, *39,* 1013–1062. The author discusses the crucial role of stage and sequence in Piagetian theory. He presents evidence from his own work on the development of the child's concept of the dream in an American (N = 90) and a non-Western (the Atayal of Formosa) sample (N = 12). There was strong evidence for an invariant sequence of stages of the dream concept in the American sample. Kohlberg argues that he has evidence for a universal sequence of development. The Atayal sample, however, is too small to be conclusive evidence. Also, the dream stages do not parallel those for the development of logical thinking.

KOFSKY, ELLEN. "A Scalogram Study of Classificatory Development. *Child Development,*" 1966, *37* (1), 191–204. A test using colored blocks was devised to examine a hierarchical theory of classification adapted from Piaget's work. It was administered to 122 four to nine year olds. Perhaps because of variations in test instructions and materials no fixed sequence of difficulty was found.

NASSEFAT, M. Etude quantitative sur l'evolution des operations intellectuelles: Le passage des operations concretes aux operations formelles. Thesis. Geneva: University of Geneva, 1963. (Also published by Delachaux and Niestle, 1963). This study comes closest to testing the basic hierarchical structure of Piagetian stages. It is discussed at some length in Chapter Two.

PASCUAL-LEONE, J. "A Mathematical Model for the Transition Rule in Piaget's Developmental Stages." *Acta Psychologica,* 1970, *32,* 301–345. This study is discussed in Chapter Two.

Index

Index

Index

M

MAC ARTHUR, R. A., 43, 122
Machine test, 28-29
MILAN, F., xi, 34, 122
Mixed Inputs: development of, 56-58; results of on Colored Blocks Test, 78-79; stages related to, 99, 101
Morrisby Shapes, 44
MURRAY, J., xi-xii, 7, 123

N

NASSEFAT, M., 19, 20-23, 123, 137

O

OLVER, R. R., 102, 121
OPPER, S., 11, 122
Organization as functional invariant, 11

P

PASCUAL-LEONE, J., 19-20, 123, 137
PIAGET, J., 11, 12, 66, 69, 70, 94, 95, 97, 98, 100, 101, 102, 104, 122, 123
Piagetian theory: analysis of, 9-16; in cross-cultural research, 9-31; and Eskimo child-rearing, 40; hierarchical structure in, 6-8; testing of, 16-23, 48, 70, 76, 82, 88; universality of, 3-6
Point Hope, Alaska, 32, 33, 34, 35, 36-37, 38, 40-41, 42, 45-47
Preoperational level, testing for, 53
PRICE-WILLIAMS, D. R., 19, 26, 123, 126, 131
Pseudo-Item procedure, 74-75
Psychological states and sequencing and stage hypotheses, 67-71

R

RAINEY, F. G., 35, 36, 123
Raven's matrices, 44, 45
Research: implications of, 94-108; psychological, of Eskimos,

42-47; relativistic interpretation of, 24; universalistic interpretation of, 24. *See also* Cross-cultural research

S

Schemata, 4
Sequencing: in analogue tasks, 80; bibliography on, 135-137; cultural effects on, 82-86, 96; hypothesis of, 15; implications of research on, 95-96; in Kentucky, 89-91; and psychological states, 67-68; results of on Colored Blocks Test, 75-76; test for hierarchy of, 20-23
Shape, attention to, 82-84
SIMON, H., 11, 123
SMITH, J., 19, 123
SPENCER, R. F., 35, 36, 39, 123
Stage: in analogue tasks, 80-81; bibliography on, 135-137; cultural effects on, 86-88; hypothesis of, 15, 17; implications of research on, 96-101; in Kentucky, 89-91; measures of, 22; onset of, 69-71; and psychological states, 67-71; results of on Colored Blocks Test, 76-78
Stanford-Binet Intelligence Scale, 43
Structures, levels of, in Piagetian theory, 12-13

T

Terman-Merrill individual vocabulary test, 43
Tests: correlations of, 31; development of, 14-15, 26-31. *See also* Colored Blocks Test
THEIL, H., 115, 123
Theory-testing, 23-26
TURNER, R., 103, 122

141

Index

V

VAN STONE, J. W., 34, 35, 41, 123
VERNON, P. E., 2, 43, 124, 128
Vest, Kentucky, 89

W

Wainwright, Alaska, 34, 37
Wechsler Intelligence Scale for Children (WISC) Block De-sign: Colored Blocks Test related to, 92-93; correlations with, 31; results of at Point Hope, 45-47
WELLER, J., 88, 124
WILEY, D., 7, 123
WILKINSON, J., 6, 124, 128
Witkin's Embedded Figures, 44
WOLFE, R., 7, 123